JOHN WESLEY
AS EDITOR AND AUTHOR

John Wesley
AS EDITOR AND AUTHOR

BY

THOMAS WALTER HERBERT

WIPF & STOCK · Eugene, Oregon

Wipf and Stock Publishers
199 W 8th Ave, Suite 3
Eugene, OR 97401

John Wesley as Editor and Author
By Herbert, Thomas Walter
ISBN 13: 978-1-55635-792-3
Publication date 1/9/2008
Previously published by Princeton University Press, 1940

CONTENTS

PREFACE

IT IS one of the chief glories of Alfred the Great that, having welded the Anglo Saxon tribes into the semblance of a nation, he labored to relieve his subjects of their woeful ignorance by initiating a revival of literary interest and activity. Curiously paralleling Alfred, John Wesley undertook the double task of moulding a chaotic mass of people into a formidable unit of God's kingdom and awakening in them an understanding of the world of ideas imprisoned in books.

Wesley's was a strange difficulty. Though a fine literary culture was thriving in England, many circumstances raised a wall between that culture and his unlearned flock. He found a way of piercing the barrier. Since it was a way completely unorthodox among the professors of literature and since most of these cultivated gentlemen cared nothing for the people whom he loved, the hewing devolved upon him alone. Singlehanded, therefore, he struck and struck again as he could find opportunity amidst the many calls of a busy life.

The result was awe-inspiring. John Wesley, open-air preacher to an ignorant mob, became also a historian, a biographer, a magazine editor, a writer of medical treatises, a producer of novels, a lexicographer, a translator of poems, a music critic, a philologist, a grammarian in half a dozen languages, a writer in natural philosophy, a poetry anthologist, a writer on logic, a political controversialist, an economist, an ecclesiastical historian, a Bible commentator, and one of the most thorough literary dictators in history. Seldom in modern times has any other man even attempted to cover so vast an intellectual field. Jack of all trades, perhaps; nor was he disposed to pretend to mastery in them—it was his voluntary task to introduce the masters to his people. And yet to many of those people he must have seemed a universal genius.

So intrinsically excellent was his taste and creative ability and so important was to become the multitude he firmly led that the influence of his pen has operated strongly upon the subsequent literature of the whole English-speaking world. From such extremes as George Eliot, the singers of American Negro spirituals, and the great poets of English Romanticism come voices modified by his.

In his *Romantic Movement and Methodism* Mr. Frederick C. Gill has admirably traced the channels through which the fervor awakened in the Evangelical Revival found its way into the flood of poetry whose epoch is customarily marked by the publication of the *Lyrical Ballads* of Wordsworth and Coleridge. John Wesley was by no means the only stimulator, nor was his the only voice, of that fervor; but he was certainly the leader who made it effective. He both checked the gushing frenzies which would have dissipated religious forces in a luxury of mere feeling, and vigorously prodded the fanaticism which would have insulated religion with a crust of moral and spiritual illiberality. Mr. Gill touches Wesley's work and apprehends its importance; but no one has hitherto made a thorough investigation of Wesley's surprisingly extensive literary production.

It would be a sterile task to put Wesley into one of the neat literary pigeonholes. Although the body of his writing is significant not only as an element in the religious revival but also as a link between a wide-spread emotional upheaval and a permanently valuable phase of literature, it must not be inferred that he fits the usual conception of a romantic. To be sure, Wesley once felt his heart strangely and supralogically warmed, an experience which might ally him in a sense with Blake, Coleridge, and Wordsworth; but it was his characteristic function to stimulate forces which he then attempted to rein by reason and law. Against antinomianism similar to Blake's, Godwin's, and Shelley's he set methodical rules of conduct; against the American revolutionaries he brought into play his own and Dr. Johnson's satire; against the Methodists who would withdraw in revolt from the Church of England he said in effect, "Over my dead body;" against diffuseness in writing he levelled the most industrious abridging pen before the *Readers' Digest;* against florid rhetoric he recommended imitation of "Mr. Addison or Dr. Swift;" and among his favorite authors were Locke and Alexander Pope.

One good thing I have earned in writing this little volume: an opportunity to make the boast implicit in thanking those who helped me. Some gave me a short while and some gave me many hours; but all were skillful and generous, and all deserve the better thanks I might return if this were a better book—particularly these: Professor Thomas H. English, Professor Gordon Hall Gerould, Mrs. T. W. Herbert, Dr. Charles Leonard Lundin, Dr. Robert D. Mayo, and Dr. Craig R. Thompson. I am, moreover, gratefully indebted to the library staffs of Drew University, Emory University, Princeton Theological Seminary, and Princeton University.

CHAPTER ONE

INTRODUCTION

ARBITRARY POWER—" John Wesley was answering those who charged him with making another pope of himself—"If by arbitrary power you mean a power which I exercise singly, without any colleagues therein, this is certainly true, but I see no hurt in it."[1] Nor did the growing thousands who were the subjects and instrument of that power see any hurt in it. Those few who protested were free to escape. But multiplied hosts of men and women recognized in Wesley's personality the same element the Earl of Kent found in King Lear's countenance—authority; and, again like Kent, they fain would call it master.

Wesley was well content to rule. He protested that power was thrust upon him unsought, and we may grant that he demonstrated logically the truth of his assertion. But if circumstances forced a scepter into his hand, his was the native gift to wield it. Wield it he did from the early days at Oxford till the day when, as the acknowledged master of his own great organization, he cheerfully lay dying.

Like many another ruler, Wesley recognized and enlisted the effective power of the printed word. Though he was unable and emphatically unwilling to control, or see anyone else control, the public press of England, he established a printing house of his own, over whose productions he did exercise absolute authority. He went farther. He made it a rule of the Conference, the organization of Methodist preachers which lives to this day, that no preacher, on pain of expulsion, might print anything whatever without his express approval. When he relaxed this rule in 1780, some of the preachers immediately burst into print with prose and verse which Wesley felt would do the Methodist cause no good.[2] He was not willing that his people should spend their money on trash; so in the next year it was again decided that no production of any preacher should be printed until Wesley had "corrected" it[3]—a term which meant anything from simply glancing over the manuscript to recasting the whole effort.

Rules like this were not usually necessary for the enforcement of discipline. One of his preachers, Joseph Benson, desiring to do a bit of independent publishing, took the precaution of consulting another preacher named Hopper. "If you should make haste to publish them," Hopper warned him, "your sermons may not meet with that approbation among Methodists which you expect. You know how we are circumstanced. If Mr. Wesley only speaks a word against them or gives them a frown, that is enough. Thousands will neither buy, see, nor read them."[4]

Power to veto he supplemented by actively directing what should be written for publication. More than one author began his work by confessing that he would never have ventured into print save for Mr. Wesley's express command. These and every other writer of early Methodism received encouragement, advice, and often personal assistance from their leader. But John Wesley was the most indefatigable writer of them all.

That Wesley was absolute master of what appeared in his original writings goes without saying. That he exercised a high degree of authority over all the writings of Methodism during his lifetime is an interesting and significant fact, but one which need not further concern us now. That he maintained an arbitrary power, a power exercised, as he said, "singly, without any colleagues therein" over the three hundred and seventy-one publications of which he was definitely the personal editor is a fact of primary importance. Absolute power inescapably bears with it absolute responsibility. Of whatever occurs, therefore, in any work which he wrote, abridged, or edited in any way, we may safely say, "John Wesley is responsible for this."

There are some exceptions to the rule, exceptions to which Wesley was quick to call attention. But his disclaimer in specific cases serves only to emphasize his readiness to assume, in general, sole responsibility. "It is usual . . . with magazine writers," he whimsically told the readers of his periodical, "to speak of themselves in the plural number: '*We* will do this.' And, indeed, it is the general custom of great men to do so. But I am a little one. Let me, then, be excused in this . . . and permitted to speak as I am accustomed to do."[5] For several years thereafter the pronoun *I* appeared consistently in editorial comment. Though the force of custom finally induced Wesley to comply with its mandates, not while he lived was the plural form anything more than a bow to the conventional. Everyone knew what single hand guided the publication.

He did not scorn advice. He invariably welcomed it, often sought it, and sometimes followed it. A favorite saying of his was, "I have been prevailed upon to" pursue such and such a course. Nevertheless, whatever action was taken, it was he who took it. His judgment, though amenable to reasonable argument or suggestion, had to be completely persuaded before he would act upon advice. Whatever influence may have been brought to bear upon him, the execution of a piece of writing or editing was his, the purpose behind it was his purpose, and the responsibility for its form was his alone.

Wesley's original writings fill many heavy volumes; but the mere bulk of his abridgments is far greater. Until we see him at work it is difficult to understand how a man as busy as he was could have brought such hundreds of volumes into accord with his own ideas of what a book should be.

The circumstances under which he performed his editorial tasks must certainly be unique in literary history. He was the itinerant *par excellence*. Seldom did he stay in one town more than a few days at a time, and often one day was the limit. Until he had reached the age of seventy he made his way about on horseback; then he reluctantly acceded to friendly entreaties and accepted a carriage. The spare moments of quiet before and after his four or five hours of sleep he customarily devoted to writing his journal, letters, controversial pieces, and other original productions. Sometimes he found opportunity in such odd moments to employ an abridging pen. But it was often the hours of actual travel on the back of his much-bestridden horse that saw him preparing other men's work for republication. It must have been a remarkable sight, however familiar it became on the highways of England: a small man in scrupulously neat clerical dress, jogging somewhat awkwardly along the road, reins hanging loose on the horse's neck, book in one hand and busy pencil in the other, marking through a word here, a phrase there, and a sentence or paragraph yonder, now and then writing in the margin or changing punctuation to suit the requirements of abbreviated sentences.

Such was the principal editorial office of Methodism for the forty years ending in 1773; and such were the means whereby many a well-thumbed book was regenerated for the glory of God and the advancement of the Societies.

Of making many books there was no end, but a closed book is a mockery of wisdom. Believing that "Reading Christians will be knowing Christians,"[6] he bent his energies toward opening books all over England. As early as 1730 he wrote to Anne Granville, a friend of his who, he thought, was in danger of piously narrowing her interests: "Yet, as nobly useful as divinity is, 'tis perhaps not advisable to confine yourself wholly to it: not only for fear it should tire one who has been used to variety of subjects, but chiefly for fear it should make you less useful to those who have the happiness of your acquaintance; for whose sake therefore, as well as your own, I should fancy you would like to intermix some history and poetry with it. 'Tis incredible what a progress you might make in all these in a year or two's time, could you have a fixed hour for each part of your work."[7]

When he organized his Methodist Societies, he set up libraries for them and urged the purchase and reading of good books wherever he went. But he was continually plagued with well-intentioned people who held that the Holy Scripture was not only the best but the only worthwhile reading. As late as 1774 he found it necessary to combat such notions: "In that and several other instances I take knowledge of Sarah Ryan's littleness of understanding: and this, as well as our temper, we ought to improve to the utmost of our power; which can no otherwise be done than by reading authors of various kinds as well as by thinking and conversation. If we read nothing but the Bible, we should hear nothing but the Bible; and then what becomes of preaching?

"Many people have clear conceptions of a few things, concerning which they judge and reason. But they have no clear ideas of other things. So, if they reason about them, they stumble at every step. None can have general good sense unless they have clear and determinate ideas of all things."[8]

"It is certain," he declared on another occasion, "the Author of our nature designed that we should not destroy but regulate our desire for knowledge."[9] Where desire for knowledge was sleeping he made it his special business vigorously to wake it.

If heredity plays a part in the formation of literary taste and creative talent, John Wesley was fortunate. Both his father and his mother were highly cultivated persons, and both sprang from generations of strong minds and forceful personalities.

The father was an indefatigable poet. A versified history of the Bible was in progress at the Epworth parsonage when John was born. Samuel Wesley's poem on the battle of Blenheim brought him an army chaplainship from the Duke of Marlborough; and interminable tomes of religious poetry brought upon his name a drop of acid in Pope's early *Dunciad.*

Susannah Wesley, daughter of the learned and eminent Dissenting minister, Dr. Annesley, assumed responsibility for the Wesley children's early education. A rigorous discipline she enforced; but, tempering her severity with an intelligent breadth of vision, she justified it by the excellence of her own sense of values and by the admirable simplicity of her own forceful gift of expression.

The literary talents of the family bore fruit in several of the children. Charles Wesley's poetic fame is attested in every Protestant hymn book. Samuel Wesley, junior, who remained an orthodox conservative in the Establishment, published a rather charming volume of poems; his friendship with Alexander Pope probably won the elimination of his father's name from the final version of the *Dunciad.* Martha Wesley, as Mrs. Hall, had an honored place in the circle of Dr. Johnson's friends. Mehetabel, unfortunate in her life as in her name, contributed to the *Arminian Magazine* a number of pathetic poems graced by a tender beauty.

John Wesley developed his native talent under as favorable a course of formal training as England afforded. Entering the Charterhouse at the age of ten years, he won distinction among his classmates and became a favorite with the master, Dr. Walker. In 1720 he matriculated at Christ Church, Oxford, and entered upon his studies with an unusual scholarly earnestness, which was rewarded in 1729 by a fellowship in Lincoln College, and election to the position of Greek Lecturer and moderator of the classes. In the following February he took the degree of Master of Arts.

A passion for exact method prompted him during his residence at Oxford, to lay out a schedule of reading and study in the various branches of conventional learning. By rigid adherence to his self-imposed duties, he "collected" an enormous number of carefully selected books from the Hebrew, Greek, Latin, French, and English literatures. When Wesley "collected" a work, he outlined it in a commonplace book, commented upon it, and transcribed such passages as seemed to him most significant and worthy of being remembered.

The literary interests thus acquired remained with him throughout life. When he was not actually working out his own projects, his countless hours on horseback were devoted to reading over his old favorites or exploring new books. Later in his life, the occasional carriage-companions of his journeys observed the same habit continuing: Horace or Spenser or Milton or some other master was usually his closest comrade except when he engaged in his ever-pleasing but somewhat rare hours of conversation.

So thoroughly did he saturate himself with the world's great literature that nearly all his writings contain, here and there, quotations so aptly used that allusiveness never halts the perspicuous flow of his language.

It was with this sort of equipment that John Wesley approached his task of creating and maintaining a dictatorship over the reading of his followers. By native gift and arduous training he was able to learn and sift critically the best that had been thought and said in the world. By virtue of his winning personality and the tremendous driving power of a consuming purpose, he was able effectively to propagate the best, as he saw it, among thousands of those who stood most in need of a competent critic.

It was not enough for Wesley merely to indicate the sources of literary beauty to his followers. Methodists were poor and unaccustomed to reading. He must provide cheap volumes to fit their financial capacities; he must provide simplified and explained writings to suit their educational limitations; and he must provide the inducement of his own name so that people who knew nothing of, say, Milton, would be impelled to buy and read Mr. Wesley's book.

How he did all that, and how much more he did in the literary world are questions to which the following pages give something of an answer.

CHAPTER TWO

THE JOURNAL

HIS JOURNAL is justly the most famous of all Wesley's writings. Largely because of it, the primary source of our information about the author's life, there are few men about whom the known facts are more complete. It enables us to track every important activity in which he was engaged—from his successful attempt to reform the religious consciousness of England to his unsuccessful attempts to find the happiness of woman's love; and we can hear of every important phenomenon he observed—from the gaping astonishment of colliers who had never before seen an open-air preacher to the faultless simplicity of Alexander Pope's poetic style.

In many ways the Journal follows typically the course of the characteristic Wesley enterprise: he prepared it with a practical purpose in view, his work was merely a thoroughly developed execution of another man's idea, he amplified his purpose into something far more significant than was envisioned in his first plan, and he incorporated it neatly into the scheme of his life's work.

Inasmuch as the work exists in three distinct states (manuscript, contemporary editions of extracts, and complete or nearly-complete editions) I shall refer to it as the Journal when I mean the work in general, irrespective of any particular form of it; as the journal, to indicate Wesley's manuscript original; as *Journal Extract,* to indicate the sections published in Wesley's lifetime; and as *Journal,* to indicate Curnock's "Standard Edition."

In 1725 Wesley lighted upon a suggestion in Bishop Jeremy Taylor's *Rules for Holy Living and Dying* that it would be well for a religious man each night to make a careful review of his actions during the day. What could be a more accurate and thorough method than to write down the employment of each hour? He began to do literally just that,[1] and very shortly keeping his record became one of the fixed habits which won for him along with his companions in righteousness the name *Methodist.*

For some time the diary continued merely as a help in Wesley's endeavors to conserve and methodize his time and to provide an objective view of his own activities so that he might eliminate his faults and nourish his precious though numerous virtues. At length, however, when he came to America in the service of the Established Church, he found himself leading a life more adventurous than he had known as a resident of Lincoln College. "The variety of scenes which I then past thro'," he said to his earliest readers, "induced me to transcribe from time to time, the more material parts of my Diary, adding here and there such little Reflections as occurr'd to my mind."[2]

This brief description announces the manner in which the Journal was born. The terms "diary" and "journal" have a specialized significance when applied to Wesley's writings.

The diary was his personal, private record. In a convenient little book which would fit into his pocket, he jotted down an extremely brief hourly notation of what occupied his days. For the double purpose of saving time and keeping his thoughts secret, he employed a peculiar combination of abbreviated longhand, cipher, and shorthand. But even when translated into correctly spelled words, the record is austerely concise. An hour of language-study would produce only a pen-scratch meaning "German"; an incident sometimes produced a sentence: "Mrs. Hawkins beat her boy,"[3] or "Oglethorpe seemed quite open, and in an excitable temper."[4] Wesley occasionally summarized a related group of happenings or preserved a memorandum of his private meditations and devotional periods; and at definite periods he reviewed the foregoing days. Here he revealed what he almost invariably avoided exhibiting in the books he published, in the sermons he preached, or in his contacts with other men: a highly introspective, self-questioning nature. The diary, therefore, is much what the term customarily signifies.

Some care must be taken to differentiate this from his journal, for "journal" is ordinarily used to indicate something not fundamentally dissimilar from a diary. The journal was a fruit of formal, literary effort. The diary, from this point of view, stood in the capacity of a body of detailed notes. With these to prompt his memory, Wesley composed a loosely connected story of the incidents he had lived through—putting the material into a form at once understandable and attractive to readers, and stiffening the narrative with "such little Reflections as occurr'd" to his mind. The work, therefore is really a studied autobiography. The calendar form may be considered not only a very convenient frame upon which an unplotted series of events might be hung, but also a literary device which would at the same time excuse the writer for saying a great deal about himself and give the work a familiar, conversational, almost confidential flavor.

As a matter of fact, the early sections of the journal were at one time used as personal letters. Wesley knew that his family and his intimate friends would be interested in the happenings which were making his life adventurous, and for his own sake he wished them to have an accurate narrative of the way he was employing his time. Instead of repeating the same thing over and over again in letters, he transcribed copies of his journal. One copy, of course, went to his home, and others went to places where he had groups of friends who would wish to take turns reading what he had written.

Shortly after he returned from the colonies, however, the journal he had made for himself and his acquaintances was put to a wider and more practical use.

During Wesley's residence in America he had at first handicapped and then utterly ruined his acceptability as a clergyman by a series of actions which speak far better for the good intentions, purity, and innocence of his heart than they do for his wisdom and sense of humor. He had insisted upon rigid ecclesiastical formalism in a community whose frontier manners were apt to rebel against such restraint; by exercising himself to the limit of his jurisdiction over the spiritual life of his flock he had incurred charges of meddlesomeness; by energetically rooting out the source of certain scandals directed against his friends he had made himself the object of feminine hate; he had comported himself with incredible innocence where a young woman was concerned and later (when she had given her preference to another man) expelled her harshly from communion; he had made the church a center of dissension; and he had hardly succeeded in compensating for the strife by productive work. As a result, he had completely exasperated many of his friends in the colony, and had made himself some good, hearty enemies. Reverberations of his folly were humming in England when he arrived at home; he found himself the object of attacks which must have cut and stung the deeper because of his consciousness of at least partial failure. Fortunately for his self-respect, their venom was tinctured with a large admixture of falsehood. He had learned enough to keep quiet under well-directed fire, but the stray shots gave him a much-needed chance to justify his actions. Conscious of the integrity of his purposes, and not by any means convinced that he had met with the justice he deserved, he rightly concluded that a sort of *apologia pro vita sua*—a true, circumstantial narration of the significant events in his thus far apparently unfortunate career—would be the soundest defense he could make. It was with this end in view that he selected large portions of his manuscript journal, arranged them anew, made a few necessary alterations, and published his first *Journal Extract.*[5]

The Georgia episodes were not the only grounds upon which Wesley had already been severely criticized. In order to clear his name of certain unjust imputations that had come as a result of his leadership over the old Oxford Holy Club, he prefaced the first *Journal Extract* with a long letter he had written to Mr. Richard Morgan, explaining the circumstances under which that gentleman's son had died, and outlining the activities of the Club.[6]

He was destined to write much more in defense of his organized religious activity. Not long after his return from America, Wesley joined the Fetter Lane Society of the Moravian Brethren and quickly gravitated to a position of leadership. As a result of this connection he experienced that famous warming of the heart in Aldersgate Street which exercised so profound an influence upon his subsequent life and indirectly upon the life of England; and he began in his preaching to emphasize doctrines which, as they would hitherto have been repugnant to him, were still highly objectionable to the authorities of the emotionally dozing English Church. He roused some sort of emotion immediately: he was vehemently and angrily attacked nearly everywhere he went. Again, therefore, he felt himself called upon to explain the remarkable circumstances which had conditioned his actions, and again he did so by publishing a *Journal Extract.*[7] But there was a new note in his voice. He was not so much concerned with excusing his actions in the eyes of assailants as with removing cause for prejudice from those who might come under his own influence. For he was now possessed by the conviction that he was able to deliver to men "that word which is able to save their souls."[8]

By the time the next *Journal Extract* appeared, in 1742, Wesley had completely broken away from the Moravians; and, with the nucleus of those who preferred his leadership and teaching, he had definitely launched out upon the course which was to occupy the rest of his many years. The name *Methodist* clung to him and now came to be applied to the rapidly increasing group who joined him in spreading the evangelical and experimental conception of a present joyful salvation through faith in Christ. He now perceived that he was, as he was glad to be, inextricably identified with Methodism, and he was aware that people considered him the embodiment of the ideals and purposes which were its core.

That identification entailed certain difficulties. He had thought it possible to draw to himself men who, knowing intimately his manner of life, might refute the evil things falsely said of him by giving the direct evidence of their own observation. It was a futile hope. "For," he confessed, "how notorious it is that, if a man dare to open his mouth in my favour, it needs only be replied, 'I suppose you are a Methodist too,' and all he has said is to pass for nothing!" He appealed to all men, therefore, to hear him speak for himself, and to hear without prejudice: "You have heard one side already; hear the other, weigh both, allow for human weakness, and then judge as you desire to be judged."[9]

Accepting the responsibility of representing Methodism in the eyes of the world, he undertook boldly what was in reality quite possible—to tell the story of the movement by giving an account of his own life. Nor did he hesitate to assume the character of a special instrument of God: "What I design in the following Extract is, openly to declare to all mankind what it is that the Methodists (so called) have done, and are doing now—or, rather, what it is that God hath done, and is still doing, in our land."[10]

Into this sweeping design had developed the early purpose of the diary. Beginning as a pedantic scheme for budgeting time and checking up on his hours to see that they were lived in the best possible fashion, the first punctilious jottings had grown into a running history and *apologia* of the most important religious and social movement of eighteenth century England. When it had reached such proportions, the future of the Journal was insured. Wesley would periodically publish Extracts from now till the last decade of the century.

Slowly but surely the *Journal Extracts* achieved the goal their author had set. Gradually Wesley won the respect of England for himself; and if that respect did not extend in equal measure to Methodism, it was not for lack of effort on his part. During the closing years of his life the churches which had previously excluded him sent more invitations than he could possibly accept. The stage, which had ridiculed his Methodists wittily and unmercifully, found it unprofitable to crack a joke at their expense. In no small degree this change resulted from the knowledge that John Wesley's life accorded with his preaching, and the *Journal Extracts* were the transparent medium through which the multiform activities of that life could be viewed.

If the *Journal Extracts* had their part in producing so salutary an effect upon the outside, how much more influential they were with the increasingly large numbers in the Societies themselves! Wesley must have been aware that as the story of his life was unfolded before them, they were inspired to emulation insofar as their capacities allowed and were drawn ever more completely to place their confidence in him as their leader.

As years went on and the Methodist Societies developed into an ever more extensive and smoothly working organization, the members were vastly encouraged by learning from Mr. Wesley's accounts what a great work they were a part of; and it was inspiriting in times of difficulty to reflect upon the recorded barriers over which Mr. Wesley had managed in some way to go.

Incidentally, Wesley employed the *Extracts* to publish his opinions on a wide variety of subjects, always with a practical end in view. Among these, works of literature occupied a prominent place. He was a voracious and widely eclectic reader, and it was his custom to write down in his Journal a short description, critical estimate, recommendation, or condemnation of each book as he completed it. How many people were thereby in any degree guided in their reading it is hard to calculate; but there frequently occurred entries concerning books which he later published in abridged form. For example, in December, 1750, he said, "I set upon cleansing Augeas's stable, upon purging that huge work, Mr. Fox's *Acts and Monuments,* from all the trash which that honest, injudicious writer has heaped together, and mingled with those venerable records which are worthy to be had in everlasting remembrance."[11] And the next year the *Book of Martyrs,* much reduced, appeared in *The Christian Library.*

As Methodist people read Wesley's Extracts, they found advice not only on literature, but on all the multitude of subjects that Wesley's interests comprehended. They were reminded of the poverty-stricken and their need for help, of smuggling and other lawless activities against which they could effectively set their faces, of the feelings of dumb animals, which they ought to treat with human kindness, of the economic evils of the liquor traffic, of the duty of Christians to be loyal to constituted government, of the benefits derivable from clean living and physical exercise, of that "execrable sum of all villainies" the slave trade, and of a thousand other things, great and small, which ought to concern them.

One further purpose, we may reasonably suppose, was the same as that which prompted Wesley to insist upon the writing of autobiographies by his preachers and helpers. In the 1744 Conference Wesley raised the question, "Should all our Assistants keep journals?" and answered it: "By all means, as well for our satisfaction as for the profit of their own souls."[12] He firmly believed in the efficacy of a good example, for he thought any good life was inevitably a practical manifestation of divine grace. His own conviction that he was such an exemplar of God's mercy—he was fond of calling himself "a brand plucked from the burning"—could hardly be called egotism; or if it was, the egotism was of an unusual sort. Egotism or not, he must have deemed his own life as good a source of inspiration and sound doctrine as those of the other men he called upon for accounts of themselves. If this is so, we are led to conclude that he intended his own record to be ranked with the other Lives he caused to be published—with Martin Luther's and the humble Sampson Staniforth's. Perhaps this intention finally outranked the apologetic and didactic purposes which he had earlier given as his guiding reasons.

The Journal, however, cannot be dismissed with merely an examination of its contemporary influences and its place in John Wesley's evangelistic program. It has been appropriated by the world of literature. By virtue of its intrinsic excellence, it has become an honored companion of Pepys' *Diary* and Walpole's *Letters*.

In order to evaluate the Journal as a specimen of creative art, we must leave the first editions and give our attention to its present form. For the great and significant bulk of new material which constitutes some of the most interesting parts of the twentieth century version we are indebted to the labors of the scholarly Rev. Nehemiah Curnock. His patient toil, his tactful perseverence, his minute care of detail, his fidelity to truth, and the sustained force with which he drove himself and his helpers to the completion of an enormous task—these are elements in an epic of scholarship.

The number of texts, both in print and in manuscript, which had to be collated, presented a sufficiently great problem. Wesley's customary title, "*An Extract of the Journal,* etc." was no mere figure of speech. His complete Journal he abridged with care equal to that he bestowed on works of other men. There were passages which would unnecessarily have offended living people, and there were others too distinctly personal to serve the purposes for which he published the work. For Curnock's "Standard Edition" a considerable part of the unabridged Journal was recovered, and those sections which had not before been made public were inserted in their proper places.[18]

Among the thorough and heavy annotations with which the edition is supplied, the most important feature is Wesley's diary. The patient editor went through the jumble of abbreviated longhand, cipher, and antiquated shorthand, and laboriously translated the whole mass into intelligible English. He was handicapped further because of the fact that though in some places the material was neat as a schoolboy's copybook, all too frequently it was slipshod as haste could make it. The diaries so shrouded with difficulties for the investigator are intensely private. How far Wesley intended that they should always remain a mystery to the world it is hard to say, for he neither destroyed them nor furnished a key for the elucidation of the whole. What was said in the portions Curnock chose not to print we do not know. We have merely his analysis of their contents and his assurance that "the student of Wesley's life returns from behind the scenes with a profounder regard than ever for the man who so frankly unveils himself."[14] A large part of the diaries, however, he prints concurrently with the journals. They serve as a running comment, showing the details of what Wesley tells in a more general fashion, and as an indication of how his mind played about bare facts as he spun out the narrative of his life.

It is therefore from the vantage point of the great "Standard Edition" that we must look upon the permanent value of the Journal.

The principal interest still resides in the strictly biographical features. John Wesley was easily among the most important and picturesque men of eighteenth-century England. His life was packed with incident well nigh as tightly as that of any contemporary whose greatness lay in moral or spiritual realms. The spiritual and intellectual adventures may be taken as of course. But from the days when he knew himself a coward before a storm at sea till the days when his utter fearlessness, combined with his physical stamina and mental alertness, saved him from death at the hands of threatening mobs, he encountered a multitude of adventures which make more absorbing reading than many a popular romance. Through hundreds of rapid pages he tells of his meetings with eminent people; of his surprisingly diversified interests in science, philosophy, history, literature, languages, and many other branches of learning and art; of his work in building his great organization and furnishing a body of literature for its members; he narrates, in short, the uncounted activities of a singularly eventful career lived squarely at the vital center of his nation's life.

His was a personality of strange aspects, but none was more strange than that which shows in his dealings with women. When he could keep the relationship on a plane of spiritual friendship, or when the women were pupils in religion, he was perfectly at ease, quite master of the situation. But the *Journal* tells of the two or three women with whom he was in love. There John Wesley was utterly at sea. He gives us as strange a series of love-stories as ever went into print. His own purity of heart and deed survived without the slightest blemish. His wisdom and his ability to act wisely in a given set of circumstances were for once hopelessly at fault.

The *Journal* narrates not only the events in which its author was prime mover. He was a recorder of the interesting things he saw, whether he participated in them or not. His clear, pungent sentences gain rather than lose in vividness for their crisp brevity. Here and there the reader comes across a novel or a play presented, as it were, through the wrong end of a telescope: the characters and happenings gain in sharpness of outline what they lose in breadth of development.

Here occur source materials for a history of philosophical, sociological, economic, political, and, of course, religious opinion. But in addition to the broad sweep of ideas we find indication of the less permanently significant but no less interesting eddies in the stream. For example, Wesley believed in the reality of ghosts, witchcraft, and the impingement of other supernatural phenomena upon the natural world. Long before he began printing stories of such things in the *Arminian Magazine,* he recorded his beliefs in the *Journal Extracts* and exemplified them by tales he had heard in one place and another.

The eighteenth century novel is deservedly famous for preserving a picture of the life of the time, and for this cause also Pepys' *Diary* is held in high regard. John Wesley's *Journal* yields to neither in accuracy or completeness of representation. Wesley was more thoroughly acquainted with England than any other man. His information extended vertically as well as horizontally. He knew the peasant and the noble, the artizan and the merchant prince, the common soldier and the bishop, the barkeeper and the great lady, the smuggler and the member of parliament, the brutalized collier and the toast of the town. No man was better able to observe English manners in all classes, and, indeed, no man better recorded them. The perils of the highway, the state of the crops, the scenery of town and country, the burden of taxation, the ribaldry of taverns, and the sophisticated chatter of the drawing room were all familiar to him; and he delineates them with that best of all methods of social satire—unvarnished accuracy.

Wesley was no socialist and no democrat. He had no panacea to offer for the reform of the social order except through appeal to the individual. And yet he was profoundly moved by the evils which he saw around him. The grinding curse of poverty without hope, the misery of disease without medical care, the futile and degrading forgetfulness of drunken stupor—these he observed and recorded. As one reads of the ghastly conditions he calmly sets forth, one thinks of the polite literature of the Augustan age—of its preoccupation with wit and the drawing-room, with polished style and common-sense, with preferments and advantageous matches. Underneath the apparent stability of the privileged classes the muck of despair was beginning to show motion. This sluggish seething Wesley saw, and its image he preserved.

The *Journal* is by no means a key to the whole history of eighteenth-century England. The great battles on land and sea, the financial booms and panics, the marvellous oratory of Parliament, and scores of phenomena which fill the pages of histories with gripping interest seldom find an echo here except insofar as the poor felt their repercussions. But he who shares the present concern for the underprivileged masses and he who is interested in the conditions which prefaced most of the significant social legislation of the past hundred and more years will find the *Journal* a worthy and absorbing document.

If there has been a really fundamental change in the social attitude of English-speaking peoples since the end of the seventeenth century, it is the growth of a willingness to recognize the value of the individual human being irrespective of his standing in the community. John Wesley was among the first men who had such a willingness. No, that states the case too passively. A sense that the individual man was infinitely valuable, merely from the fact of his humanity, was an integral and dominating part of the religious conviction which furnished the driving force of his whole life. So far as he was able he transmitted this passion of his to other men. That he measurably succeeded in doing so is doubtless the most important consequence of his career. But its importance for us at the moment lies in the fact that through the placid rapidity of the *Journal's* pages this sense abides and finds innumerable practical exemplifications. In a day when a poor man, in the eyes of the cultivated world, was a mere atom in the body of a great beast, or, at best, a caricature of a human being, John Wesley wrote in such a manner as to make his characteristic symbol of respect appropriate: when a poor man thanked him for a favor, he always removed his hat.[15]

CHAPTER THREE

THE LETTERS

IN THEIR OWN PECULIAR WAY the Letters of John Wesley are as interesting as the *Journal.* There is, in their widely diversified tone, ample compensation for the disconnected character inevitable in a book of collected correspondence. In this respect the Letters have some advantage over the more smoothly-running *Journal,* for they fully display those contrasts of temper which make the single-minded Wesley appear to us as something finer than the mere embodiment of a great moral and religious force. He was in reality an eminently human, affectionate, and lovable gentleman. All too often, even as self-portrayed in the *Journal,* he seems aloof from mankind, a sort of unfeeling engine who transmitted a new power to men. But human nature does not derive force from a machine. Surely there must have been something winning in the nature of one who, depending even more on personal contact than on his undoubtedly great gift of oratory, made hosts of Englishmen unflinchingly loyal to him.[1]

There was. Inasmuch as those who both heard him talk and read his letters asserted that he wrote as he spoke, it would seem reasonable to assume that in his correspondence we might discover something which would enable us to understand, at least in part, why his followers so readily obeyed him, why many who had hated and feared him were quite captured by his charm after a short conversation, and why Dr. Samuel Johnson would have been delighted to "talk all day and all night too" with him. Such, indeed, is the case. One comes from a reading of the Letters with a feeling that it would have been pleasant to know their writer, and with a more unusual feeling: that John Wesley would have been glad to know him.

Not many of these letters were wrought with studied care. They are far removed from that epistolary style and form which make the letters of Chesterfield, Walpole, and Pope a source of pleasure. These men approached their compositions in the spirit of conscious art, working them out in that atmosphere of leisure and solitude which, according to Dr. Johnson, is the necessary condition of good letter-writing. Sometimes, particularly in his more youthful days, Wesley wrote "labored" letters. But the naturalness of his later correspondence is spontaneous. "I never think of my style at all," he asserted; "but just set down the words that come first. Only when I transcribe any thing for the press, then I think it my duty to see every phrase be clear, pure, and proper."[2]

A considerable number of the extant letters were published during his lifetime. Many were addressed to current magazines and papers, discussing controverted matters, answering questions about the Methodists or about himself in his public character, or replying to assailants of various kinds; and some of his pamphlets were in the form of letters. But a vast majority were addressed to individuals, and designed for their eyes only. Scores of these he later published in *The Arminian Magazine* along with letters received from his many correspondents; and some were made public by the recipients.

His attitude toward the publication of material he had not revised for the press he stated under peculiar circumstances. A certain Richard Tompson had written to him in so intelligent a fashion as to precipitate a correspondence extending over some months. Tompson, finding himself in need of money, applied to Wesley for permission to publish what had passed between them. "I do not object," was the answer. "Only it would be needful to advertize the readers that what I wrote was in haste, just as I could snatch a little time now and then, to answer the private letter of a private friend, without any thought of its going farther."[3]

From time to time after Wesley's death, selections from his letters found their way into print, but it remained for the late John Telford, who had ably assisted Curnock with the *Journal,* to issue, in 1931, an edition which is a fitting companion for the earlier work. All the known collections were put to use, and single letters were sent in to the editor from all parts of the world. These, together with what had already been printed, brought the total number to 2,670 by the time the eight volumes of the "Standard Edition" went to press. Very probably more will come to light in the future, but there doubtless will be few highly significant additions.

The Letters open with a communication from Oxford to the treasurer of the Charterhouse. Wesley may be seen making a stilted but careful explanation of a financial mistake that had occurred while he was at his old school.[4] Thereafter the young Oxonian rapidly developed a style of writing which fits pat into the picture we know of him as a brilliant, cultivated young man, gaining the respect of his preceptors and the respect and friendship of his companions. A straightforward assurance is already manifest, but a certain allusiveness and breadth in his paragraphs suggests that he has not yet begun to train himself in the severe simplicity which is later to characterize his style. An academic, leisurely charm pervades the long epistles, a desire to give pleasure as well as information, a tendency to revel in sound and form.

Most of the Oxford letters were written to members of his own family, and the second largest group comprises his correspondence with that Mrs. Pendarves who, born Mary Granville, was afterwards the Mrs. Delaney so well known in Dr. Johnson's literary circle, and to Mrs. Pendarves' sister Ann Granville. With these people Wesley naturally had a community of interests and tastes which gave him broad opportunities for self-expression. He drew upon his wide reading in contemporary literature and his familiar companions the classics; he touched lightly and somewhat awkwardly upon romance and indulged his talent in verse-making. The result is doubly charming in contrast with the purposeful single-mindedness of his later writing.

These days of apparent serenity were not to last long. The question of a permanent career had to be faced and evaded; then came the expedition to Georgia. The letters follow the broadening horizon and begin to show something of business-like directness. During this time and the period wherein his life work definitely took shape, the style develops rapidly; by the time he got the reins of the Methodist Societies well in hand, the terseness, the extraordinary combination of transparent clearness and parsimonious brevity, the abrupt directness and crisp authority of his characteristic manner have become habitual.

Not that Wesley's letters are all in one fashion. Far from it. In many ways the most adaptable of men, he made his mode of expression vary with the educational background of his correspondents. In letters to his brother and other university men he continued his old habit of dropping into Latin or Greek when an apt phrase from these languages occurred to him. In writing to the unlearned he did indeed maintain correctness, dignity, and purity. But he not only avoided classical allusion: he achieved a simplicity of diction, a shortness of sentence-structure, and a perspicuity of expression such as would be understandable to a child.

In these surface matters there is not a whit more variation than in a more subtle and fundamental quality which may be called tone. Delicately, unerringly, Wesley tuned his instrument to suit the occasion. Every good writer does that in some measure; no one will be surprised to see formal elaborateness following his address to Bishop Warburton as "My Lord,—" nor the familiar, playful seriousness with which he follows up his "Dear Sammy,—". But the sensitive reader would almost undertake to sketch the personality of each man who received one of Wesley's letters. He could be tender or peremptory, conversational or commanding, conciliatory or abrupt, humorous or solemn, encouraging or acid. But these and any other sets of contrasts are insufficient to indicate the amazing flexibility of his voice.

There is a perfectly good explanation of it. Each person with whom he came in contact was important in his eyes and held a singular and special place in his regard. When he wrote a letter, he thought not of himself or his style; he forgot himself and deliberately and habitually held his correspondent before his mind's eye. In reality, therefore, the highly diversified tone of his letters is another manifestation of that genius for the individual which was the keystone of Wesley's power and the very essence of his religion.

The controversial epistles, though they filled their proper niche in Wesley's great scheme, served so specialized a purpose as to set them apart from the bulk of what is left to us. The others, those not touched with controversy, performed a still more important function. They were the nerves in the body of Methodism. By means of them Wesley maintained his directing and vitalizing contact with the very extremities of his organization. "It is a rule with me," he said, "to answer all the letters which I receive."[5] No question his humblest follower asked was too small for his sympathetic attention. A woman, for instance, who wondered about the moral implications of having a flower garden received his grave assurance, backed by a demonstration based on Scripture, that such an occupation was by no means inconsistent with Christian living, but, rather, a commendable way to spend one's time.[6]

The habit of attending to details was characteristic of his leadership. He heard, apparently, that certain property near Newcastle was being allowed to fall into disrepair; he wrote to those in charge specifically directing what should be done even down to naming the place where gooseberries, currants, and strawberries should be planted.[7]

Some of his preachers were prone to show more zeal than wisdom in their manner of achieving emphasis; patiently and persistently he wrote to them in words which revolved about the injunction, "Don't scream!"[8]

Such minor matters take their humble place beside the major cares of Methodism in Wesley's letters. Provision for families of preachers, the necessity for pastoral visitation and relief of the poor, questions of doctrine and what ought to be preached, the allocation of preachers to suitable circuits, and the moral problems of perplexed people in real difficulties called forth Wesley's advice, command, or exhortation. By means of letters he kept emphasizing the means whereby his cause could be extended and its work made perfect. He would plead for interest in the distribution of books, for a firm stand against smuggling, and for a spirit of brotherhood. He would caution his people against the dangers of increasing wealth, and his preachers against aping the proud ways of gentlefolk. He would encourage the growth of Sunday Schools or rejoice in a fine bit of congregational singing. In all these things he was profoundly interested; and where a definite response was desired he was almost invariably able to strike the right, the effective note.

These episcopal duties are biographically and historically important, but there is also, in the Letters, a wealth of interesting facts about numerous spheres of Wesley's interests and activities, which are nowhere else available. One who reads only the *Journal* might conclude that he was careless of the political affairs of England; the letters correct such an impression. In his capacity as a citizen he wrote to Lord North, pleading for just government in America.[9] When all England was fearful of a French invasion, he offered to raise a company of volunteers.[10] At the very end of his life he wrote a letter, his last, to the crusading Wilberforce, encouraging him in his political fight to end the slave trade.[11]

The Letters are, in fact, a necessary supplement to the *Journal.* They begin the story of his life at an earlier point than the *Journal.* But we also may hear him speaking frankly about himself concerning matters which the other kind of writing would not call forth. That is not to say that he exhibited, even in letters, his highly introspective nature. He observed himself as he observed others, looking rather at the overt result than at the machinery of his mind. For example, after one of his preachers had talked with him about literary and oratorical style, Wesley thought over the conversation and wrote a series of letters, setting forth at some length not only his idea of what constituted a good style but also an analysis of his own.[12] The accuracy of his observation of himself and his judgment of his own literary rank are, it may be added, well nigh unexceptionable, so far as they go.

In a peculiar way, the Letters stand as a supplement to all Wesley's other writings. The hundreds of books he published were addressed to groups or to the general public. That fact was inescapable, no matter how directly he spoke to the reader; and what was said had to be expressed in more or less general terms. The Letters have, by and large, the same tenor as the rest. But in them the general conception, argument, or bit of advice is modified and interpreted in the light of Wesley's understanding of the personality of his individual correspondent.

CHAPTER FOUR

THE CHRISTIAN LIBRARY

"I HAVE OFTEN THOUGHT of mentioning to you and a few others," wrote Wesley to a friend in 1748, "a design I have had for some years, of printing a little library, perhaps of fourscore or one hundred volumes, for the use of those that fear God. My purpose was to select whatever I had seen most valuable in the English language and either abridge or take the whole tracts, only a little corrected or explained, as occasion should require."[1]

Thus casually did he announce his most extensive venture in book editing. Biographers have not spared adjectives in describing its magnitude; and, indeed, "prodigious" and "Herculean" seem scarcely hyperbolical in view of all he had on his hands. But Wesley's placid manner was no mere pose: he took *The Christian Library* in his normal stride. Unaccustomed to dawdle with any undertaking, he proceeded to add to the books he had already prepared for the purpose, so that the very next year witnessed the printing of one volume. By that time he had his complete design well organized. The work was to appear in fifty duodecimo volumes of something over three hundred pages each. Progress was rapid, and in 1755 the last nine volumes left the press.[2]

In many respects the work was a dismal failure. Despite all efforts for distribution through the channels of a highly efficient organization, and in spite of his own earnest recommendations, the sale was slow. Wesley was constrained to seek a time-worn literary consolation in hoping that "Perhaps the next generation may know the value of it."[3] So futile a resort was rare in him. But it was no more rare than the experience of unintentionally sustaining a financial loss from a book: even at the end of the year 1752 *The Christian Library* was proceeding under a deficit of above two hundred pounds;[4] and there is no evidence that it ever paid for itself. Most disappointing of all, the *Library* was itself an intrinsically faulty performance.

Wesley made it a point of pride never to allow himself haste. "I have no time to be in a hurry," he said in later years.[5] If he had needed experience to teach him that lesson, *The Christian Library* gave it to him with a vengeance. His habit in abridging was to furnish the printer with the original volume of a work through which he had gone, scratching out passages to be deleted and writing other necessary alterations between the lines or in the margins. This was his procedure with *The Christian Library.* The printers and correctors of the press, either through their own carelessness or through inevitable misunderstanding of Wesley's markings, left in the text "a hundred passages" which he had meant to exclude.[6]

Enemies pounced gleefully on the *Library* and found therein material for a telling fusillade. One day he heard a man in the street vociferously hawking a doctrinal tract and bawling "the Rev. John Wesley" as its author. The title was unfamiliar; so he secured and read a copy. He remembered having seen something like the contents before, but the doctrines were by no means those he taught. In order to counteract possible ill effects he shortly thereafter published a pamphlet setting forth what he really did maintain on the subject and mentioning the occurrence which prompted his action. The trap was ready, and he could not have put his foot more squarely into it. The former publication came out in a second edition with this statement: "There is not the least fraud in the publication nor imposition on Mr. Wesley; for the words are transcribed from the ninth and tenth volumes of his *Christian Library.*"[7]

Wesley had too highly developed a sense of humor not to see that the joke was distinctly on him. But inasmuch as the matter was serious, he considered an answering explanation necessary; and inasmuch as there was an element of disingenuousness in his assailant, he felt at liberty to season his reply with pepper. "*The Christian Library,*" he pointed out, "is not Mr. Wesley's writing: it is 'Extracts from and Abridgments of' other writers; the subjects of which I highly approve, but I will not be accountable for every expression. Much less will I *father* eight pages of I know not what which a shameless man has picked out of that work, tacked together in the manner he thought good, and then published in my name. He puts me in mind of what occurred some years since. A man was stretching his throat near Moorfields and screaming out, 'A full and true account of the death of the Rev. George Whitefield!' One took hold of him and said, 'Sirrah! what do you mean? Mr. Whitefield is yonder before you.' He shrugged up his shoulders, and said, 'Why, sir, an honest man must do something to turn an honest penny.' "[8]

It was true, nevertheless, that *The Christian Library,* even when not tampered with in the manner of this ingenious abridger of abridgments, contained perfectly obvious and flagrant contradictions of what had appeared in Wesley's own writings; and he was forced in all honesty to admit that the fault probably did not lie wholly with the printers and correctors.[9] Notwithstanding his stout denials of agreeing with every statement in the compilation, and notwithstanding his explanations of how the accident occurred, he was obviously as chagrined as it was possible for him to be. He may have protested that the writings were not his own and that the questionable passages would be counterbalanced by the force of his own writings. But the fact remained that he had undertaken to purge the works of error and had failed to do so. By setting his hand to the task of abridging he inevitably entailed responsibility for the result; and people had a perfectly sound right to father him with it.

After all this has been said, however, it must be added that the actual quantity of objectionable matter he had permitted to remain was relatively quite small; and once the damage had been done he applied the only appropriate remedy: he warned readers against the offending passages. He also eventually corrected the *Library* with great care. But the result was not made public until after his death.

In spite of its defects (as well as partially because of them), *The Christian Library* furnishes a most illuminating revelation of Wesley's editorial methods and purposes. By virtue of magnitude alone it would be in some degree important; but it has better claims on the attention.

Wesley was determined that his Methodist people should be a reading people. "Reading Christians," he was fond of repeating, "will be knowing Christians." Well aware of the transitory impression made by mere preaching, he bent great efforts to conserve the resolutions so induced. Two principal means to that end were organization—whereby the people might encourage each other to persevere in the common purpose—, and continual reading—whereby the entering wedge of the spoken word might be driven home and made to find permanent lodgment.[10]

Naturally, books of divinity (practical divinity, as he called it) held first place in his design. He was convinced that no language held a better and more extensive store of such writings than the English. But the very multitude of books—row on row of imposing folios—constituted their own effective barricade against investigation. Granted that a man wanted to read, where would he begin in this bewildering mass of material, and how would he know what to choose, once he had begun, in order that he might best profit by his labor?[11]

Moreover, as Wesley thought, even in the best books there was usually more said than was worth a man's time to read. Sometimes this was mere padding or repetition of what had been said better elsewhere. Sometimes there was much falsehood intermingled with the truth, "so (casually or designedly) blended together that it is not an easy thing to separate." And sometimes the superfluous material was controversy, an element not only commonly grown out of its usefulness but actually harmful in its tendency to stir up disputings among people who ought rather to work in harmony.[12]

The inherent difficulty of some valuable books made them unserviceable to ordinary men. On the one hand, they came from writers whose thoughts were couched in language so learned as to be practically unintelligible to all but the erudite. Wesley had some sympathy with such authors: it is natural for them, he granted, "to imagine, that what is plain to themselves must needs be so to their readers also."[13] With mystics, on the other hand, he had little patience. These, he thought, were men who "seek mysteries in the plainest truths, and make them such by their explications." He believed even the most profound truths of religion to be the plainest and clearest things in the world; the language, therefore, which expresses them ought also to be so simple that the wayfaring man, though a fool, might understand it.[14]

Ironically enough, in the light of subsequent events, Wesley's final criticism of the great divines was levelled against their contradictions. "One bids us go on; another, stop; one directs us to the right hand, another to the left; insomuch that unless the reader be endued, not only with a good understanding, but with some experimental knowledge of the things of God, he is in danger of being quite bewildered. Nay, some unhappy men have been induced hereby to throw away all religion; imagining that there was nothing therein but jargon and self-inconsistency."[15]

In view of the multiplicity and inequality of available books, Wesley resolved to choose the best among them for the use of his preachers and his more earnest laymen; and in view of the verbose and unequal character of even the choice volumes, he determined to "extract the gold out of these baser mixtures."[16] The magnitude of his undertaking and his belief in its great importance induced him to seek advice. He wrote to the great Dissenting minister Philip Doddridge, requesting him to make out a list of books suitable for a course of reading. Doddridge replied with a carefully selected series. With these and other suggestions to supplement his own ideas, Wesley mapped out his table of contents. Then, in his own unique fashion he proceeded to lop off excrescences. He endeavored to produce a result which would be at once profound and intelligible, which would, avoiding all controversy and all mystical intricacies, lead men to a practical execution of Christian principles, and which would have such a consistency and integrity of purpose as would make incidental contradictions impossible.[17]

In consideration of his stated aim, he felt no bond of fidelity to any author. He not only omitted what he saw fit, but added what was necessary, "either to clear their sense, or to correct their mistakes." A religious conviction was the governor of his literary conscience: "I therefore take no author for better, for worse; (as indeed I dare not call any man Rabbi;) but endeavour to follow each so far as he follows Christ. And not (knowingly) one step farther."[18]

His failure to insure consistency was not the only target Wesley's *Library* set up for hostile fire. But elsewhere he was less vulnerable. "Is not your *Christian Library* an odd collection of mutilated writings of Dissenters of all sorts?" So ran one question. "No," he replied. "In the first ten volumes there is not a line from any Dissenter of any sort; and the greatest part of the other forty is extracted from Archbishop Leighton, Bishops Patrick, Ken, Reynolds, Sanderson, and other ornaments of the Church of England."[19] Some of the writers he had followed were, indeed, of other denominations. He was delighted with the opportunity of admitting the fact and supplementing his retort with a declaration of intellectual independence and tolerance not only true but well calculated to appeal to Englishmen. "I mind not who speaks," he snapped, "but what is spoken."[20]

The *Library* opened with a selection from the *Epistles* of the apostolic fathers of the Church, whom Wesley, in agreement with the traditional view, held worthy of "only little less regard than . . . the sacred writings" of the scriptural canon.[21] In accordance with the promise of the title, most of the succeeding works were of a more or less similar cast, but there was some variety even in this exclusively religious literature. Sermons, letters, books of devotion, and writings of divers other types were interspersed among the most numerous class, which one may follow Wesley in calling "treatises".

There were many biographies. Notable was a long section comprising Clark's *Lives of Eminent Men* and supplementary *Lives* from several other authors. Others were within the somewhat vague line which delimits the special *genre* of the Saints' Lives. The first volume contained martyrdoms of St. Polycarp and St. Ignatius, and the next four volumes were composed largely of extracts from the famous *Acts and Monuments of the Christian Martyrs.* Wesley thought by this means to demonstrate the effect of religion upon the conduct of a man's life—to show "Christianity reduced to practice."[22]

A curious extension of Wesley's purpose that the *Library* should show the practical workings of Christianity may be seen in volume XXII. There he prints a treatise called *Directions for Married Persons: Describing the Duties common to both, and peculiar to each of them,* by William Whateley. It was a subject upon which Wesley himself might have profitably received some really sound advice.

In pursuance of his determination to "mind not who speaks but what is spoken," he included in *The Christian Library* certain works not originally constructed upon a primarily religious design; such, for example, were the five essays by Abraham Cowley in volume XXXII. Some of the distinctively religious writings, on the other hand, belong also to the permanent treasury of literature: Pascal's *Thoughts* and Bunyan's other great allegory, *The Holy War,* for example, could not remain the exclusive property of strictly religious readers.

Most of the separate works in *The Christian Library* have a preface of one sort or another. Usually there is at least a short biographical sketch of the author. Sometimes there is a critical estimate of the writing itself. These accounts frequently occur in Wesley's own incisive sentences, but more often they, as well as the articles they introduce, are the work of other men. For one who wishes to know what Wesley thought about a certain author, the edited prefaces are fairly reliable. But it seems a pity that he did not more often take time to give his own critiques; for when they do appear, their raciness and their independence of the usual trite estimates is always interesting, often quite refreshing, and sometimes startlingly sound.

CHAPTER FIVE

THE ARMINIAN MAGAZINE

MEMBERS of the Church of England in the eighteenth century were allowed a considerable latitude in theological belief. One of the more striking differences of opinion among orthodox churchmen was that which hinged upon the nature of God's omnipotence. The opposing groups looked back upon Calvin and Arminius, respectively, as their most significant spokesmen; but that neither of these great thinkers had said the last word for his position was a belief attested by increasing thousands of controversial pages.

The basis of admission to John Wesley's societies was only by implication an acceptance of any specific doctrines at all. It was rather a certain religious attitude. Over and over again Wesley repeated his motto of intellectual tolerance, "I think and let think." Nor was this an empty formula. Many of the men who worked most faithfully with him differed profoundly in theological opinion. The name of George Whitefield is so often, and rightly, linked with his that the uninformed frequently confuse their identities; yet in some beliefs they were irreconcilably opposed to each other.

In spite of his resolute tolerance of opinion, Wesley was unwilling that his people should be drawn into doctrines which would interfere with their living an active moral and spiritual life. He was convinced that the logical consequence of the dogma of absolute and unconditional predestination could only be antinomianism and quietism; and against these enemies of moral living and active purpose he set his foot like iron. He did not consider it likely that many who had been indoctrinated with Calvinism should be converted to Arminianism, but he did think it possible by dint of argument to preserve the more practically stimulating beliefs of men who thought as he did, against the clever dialectics of the Calvinists.

It is easy but unjust to fall into the view that Wesley was unalterably opposed to Calvinism in the lump. He believed that the whole Calvinistic doctrine did not err far from the Scriptural revelation. It was only against the doctrine of the "horrible decree" that he levelled his broadsides.[1]

Since the collapse of the Licensing Act in 1688, and more particularly since the days of the *Tatler* and the first *Spectator,* English periodical journals had increased rapidly in popularity until in the seventeen-seventies there was a reading public wide enough to support a number of such publications. They served divers purposes, ranging from the dissemination of general intelligence to the enforcement of opinion by special interests, political and other.

Proponents of religious doctrines had followed the lead of Whig and Tory. In 1777 there were two periodicals, *The Spiritual Magazine* and *The Gospel Magazine,* whose editorial policy was to spread Calvinistic doctrines. It was not only on doctrinal grounds that Wesley objected to them. In addition to maintaining their principles by straightforward arguments, they had launched personal attacks against men who held contrary opinions. They had published injurious statements about Wesley himself and naturally refused him room in their pages for an answer. With acrimony Wesley charged: "They have paid no more regard to Good-nature, Decency, or Good-manners, than to Reason or Truth. All these they set utterly at defiance. . . . They have defended their dear Decrees with Arguments worthy of Bedlam, and with Language worthy of Billingsgate."[2]

In order to neutralize the effect of *The Spiritual Magazine* and *The Gospel Magazine,* Wesley determined to fight back with the Calvinists' own weapons. "I oppose magazine to magazine," he thundered.[3] Accordingly, in January, 1778, there appeared a new monthly periodical: *The Arminian Magazine: Consisting of Extracts and Original Treatises on Universal Redemption,* each number of which was an octavo booklet of about fifty or sixty pages.

Wesley prepared the magazine with an eye to permanence. As a result of his insistence upon the use of good paper, even the earliest volumes are still quite white and in excellent condition. His foresightedness was more than justified. Although the name has been altered twice, and though the size and policies have also been changed, Wesley's official Methodist periodical has outlived other similar ventures. As *The Wesleyan Methodist Magazine,* it has today the longest record of continuous publication of all the religious journals in the world.

The primary purpose of the first editor is clearly stated in his title: it was intended positively to enforce that doctrine of free grace which was the foundation of Wesley's teaching. There were to be printed, of course, none of the personal attacks which he so heartily deplored. Moreover, as he insisted, "This Magazine not only contains no railing, but (properly speaking) *no* controversy. . . . It goes straight forward, taking notice of no opponent, but invariably pursuing the one point."[4] Wesley drew a distinction between writings on controverted subjects and actual controversy. By controversy he meant writing or speaking specifically in opposition to statements made by an individual proponent of a conflicting opinion.

In the general address to the reader at the beginning of the first issue Wesley outlined the program he had in mind. "Each number," he promised, "will . . . consist of four parts: First, a defense of that grand Christian Doctrine, 'God willeth all men to be saved, and to come to the knowledge of the truth.' Secondly, an extract from the Life of some holy man, whether Lutheran, Church of England man, Calvinist, or Arminian. Thirdly, accounts and letters containing the experiences of pious persons, the greatest part of whom are still alive; and, Fourthly, verses explaining or confirming the capital doctrine we have in view."[5]

In the early months of its life the magazine quite rigidly conformed to its outlined plan. There were men among Wesley's associates who doubted the wisdom of his continuing to emphasize a doctrine upon which there was so sharp a cleavage. Though a favorite saying of his was that "God made practical divinity necessary; the devil, controversial," yet the devil was a very real and potent personality to him; and when the devil made a thing necessary it was unequivocally necessary. Consequently, he persisted in his design; he made the leading article in each number an assertion of the distinctive tenet of Arminianism.

The sections devoted to biography and "accounts and letters containing the experience of pious persons" were a new departure in magazine writings. Their congruence with the theological design of the whole might not appear obvious. But Wesley believed that if an unprejudiced person were placed in possession of an accurate narrative of a good man's life, he would be convinced that the cause of such goodness was the operation of God's spirit in his heart—an operation exclusively consistent with the nature of God as taught by Arminius.

Significantly enough, the first biography in the magazine was also the first theological treatise: Wesley's abridgment of a Life of Arminius. True to his promise, Wesley entirely disregarded denominations when he chose men whose lives should edify his readers. Nor did he stop at sex, nationality, or social station. An archbishop of the Establishment and an illiterate French serving-maid he introduced in succession,[6] patently believing them equally favored with the grace of God and equally exemplary in the conduct of their lives. But before long, biographies and autobiographies of Methodist preachers and other prominent workers in the Societies began to appear, and though these did not exclude the rest, they eventually outnumbered the Lives in any other single category.

The letters, in large measure, served a purpose similar to that of the biographies. Men and women in large numbers wrote to their spiritual adviser, telling their troubles and joys, their problems and triumphs. Some of them wrote of situations wherein they had witnessed the power of religion to convey consolation and strength. Among communications of this kind loomed large the number which proved Wesley's proud boast, "Our people die well." The writers of even the quite personal ones had no objection to their publication. As John Telford said, "For a Methodist a place in the Magazine was something like a niche in the Abbey for a statesman or a poet."[7]

But the biographical and autobiographical letters were but a part of the whole collection. Others were written by Wesley's helpers, telling of the advancement of religious work or calling attention to the dangers of its retrogression. Others came from the steadily increasing number of the regular clergy who were in sympathy with the Methodist movement, discussing various religious questions or giving encouragement to their unbeneficed fellow-workers. Still others dealt with those social problems, such as slavery, prison conditions, and education of the poor, which had already begun to feel the ameliorating impact, directly or indirectly, of Wesley's interested labors.

The editor did not keep his promise that the magazine should entirely eschew controversy. Personal attacks which appeared in hostile publications he continued to answer, when he thought an answer necessary, in journals whose policy it was to open their columns impartially. But he found in his own magazine a potential weapon. He was reluctant to use it, but he did hold it ready for emergency. "I have been frenquently attacked by the Monthly Reviewers," he said by way of warning, "but I did not answer because we were not on even ground; but that difficulty is now over: whatever they object in their *Monthly Review* I can answer in my monthly Magazine; and I shall think it my duty so to do when the objection is of any importance."[8] Accordingly, among the letters which appeared above his own signature, there occasionally came one which, as he would himself have admitted, was controversial.

Eventually, moreover, Wesley in his editorial capacity himself initiated some few attacks, chief of which were levelled against the mystical writers Behmen and Swedenborg. And he gave no more room for reply by their followers than the *Monthly Review* accorded him. It is but fair to recall, however, that *The Arminian Magazine* was never supposed to be impartial. In this respect it was like *The Gospel Magazine* and *The Spiritual Magazine,* against which Wesley never inveighed simply for their failure to print his replies. And it is but fair to add that he never, as editor, launched personal attacks against living men except in their capacity as representatives of ideas which he deplored.

Those of his own letters which he printed were only very rarely controversial. A much larger body were replies to friendly letters that he had received. There were, in addition, extracts from his pastoral correspondence and from his correspondence with friends who labored in fields where he held a common interest. Consequently, his prevailing tone was not even defensively controversial. Disputation was important in its place, for error and falsehood had to be cleared away before positive religious values could be inculcated. But since Wesley was determined that his Magazine should be a constructive force, he consistently selected for publication such of his own letters as would reinforce the tendency of the whole epistolary section: to build and strengthen in his readers a living, active faith.

The last pages of every number of *The Arminian Magazine* were, as Wesley had promised, devoted to poetry. He believed with that much-maligned critic John Dennis that if poetry is the language of the emotions, and if the sublimity of poetry is dependent upon the sublimity of its subject, then, since the religious emotion is the most powerful and universal of all, the sublimest poetry will be that which treats religious topics. Furthermore (they believed), since Christianity is the sublimest possible conception of religion, Christian poetry ought to be the sublimest possible poetry.[9] The example of John Milton was an indication of what heights might be so reached.

At first the poetry section of the magazine consisted of strictly religious verse. In fact, during the earliest months the subjects were almost exclusively such as would, at least by implication, enforce Arminian doctrines. Gradually, however, the rigid limits of Wesley's promise were relaxed until in September of 1779 he shocked his pious flock by reprinting Prior's "Henry and Emma." It is rather amusing to picture the consternation in many a godly family when the blessed Mr. Wesley's magazine, the source of doctrinal food and devotional inspiration, the mouthpiece of that saint whose holiness of countenance had been sufficient to turn murderous blows aimed at his venerable head into bewildered and uncomprehending caresses—when *The Arminian Magazine,* in short, brought fourteen pages of secular and therefore sinful pleasure into the walls of the Methodist home. Such a buzzing whirred about the editor's head from those who articulately shuddered, that he was constrained to make an apology in the preface to the succeeding volume. It is a barbed apology. "It is granted," he confessed, "it is not strictly religious. But it must be granted on the other side," he continued, with his characteristically incisive habit of laying down numbered reasons, "(1.) That there is nothing in it contrary to religion, nothing that can offend the chastest ears. (2.) That many truly religious men and women have both read and profited thereby; and (3.) That it is one of the finest poems in the English tongue, both for sentiment and language; and whoever can read it without tears, must have a stupid and unfeeling heart." He concluded his remarks, however, with the concession: "I do not know that any thing of the same kind will appear in any of the following Magazines."[10]

Perhaps he may not have known it at the time he wrote, but he was not to wait long before expanding his poetic menu again. Religious verse continued to be the staple; but epigrams of Martial in translation appeared along with specimens of the later classicism of Dryden and Pope; Shakespeare and Gray mused upon the transitory glory of life; Chaucer, in Dryden's modernization, and Cowper drew pictures of the good parson; Samuel Johnson and John Gay appeared in company with poets like Byrom and Gambold, who are seldom heard of, and poets whose names never have been heard of in the secular world and never will be.

Wesley's procedure with the magazine is typical of his peculiar genius. Time and again he took an idea, sometimes original with himself but more often borrowed, and put it to use. By watching it grow he learned its capabilities. Where it rubbed harshly against other and more important schemes, he trimmed it down; if any part proved useless or harmful, he lopped off the offending member. Thus did he make the product of his cultivation fit into the grand design. A sure sense guided him, furthermore, in developing and expanding the ideas he employed. He not only fed the productive elements so that they might grow to the full extent of their effectiveness; he engrafted fresh material to replace what he had pruned away, and by this means he made the organism bear new fruit.

Within the sections which had been announced in the first number there occurred a development which broadened the usefulness of *The Arminian Magazine.* But Wesley was not long in departing from the still rather narrowly plotted course of his table of contents. As a matter of fact, the addition of a poetry section had already started the expansion which was inevitable with any institution he laid his hand to. The subscription proposals, published in the year before the first number appeared, had provided for no poetry. Between that time and the first day of January, 1778, Wesley had consulted with unnamed friends (among whom it requires no great shrewdness to guess that his brother Charles was chief), and decided upon the inclusion of verse. After a year or two of at least nominal adherence to the plan outlined at the launching, new kinds of articles began to relieve what was really becoming a monotony.

That a man of seventy-five years should undertake the establishment of a new periodical, that he should assume the direction of its business management and popularization,[11] that he should shoulder the whole editorial responsibility, sharing with his poet-brother only the judgment of what verse should appear, may not seem altogether wonderful; for printing and distributing organizations were already in his control, he had gained vast experience in the employment of the press, and the religious principles which were to govern his editorial policy had been guiding him for forty years. But for an octogenarian to be lifting his magazine out of its set grooves instead of letting it sink in more deeply, to be leading young men and women thereby, as far as he could, away from the narrow pietism which had been one of the reflex concomitants of his own teaching, to be opening new fields in spite of his amusing assertions that he was too old for aught but carrying on in the familiar paths, that is indeed worthy of admiration. Most remarkable of all is the fact that one has to keep an eye on a chronological table to remain aware of his advanced years. He did occasionally propose his age as a reason for wishing people to leave him alone. But his accustomed vigor of manner belied his words. Critics refused to allow him the pity of senility, and even today we are not tempted to be lenient with him on that account. We can afford to treat all his work in literature as objectively as if he never passed beyond the full strength of his maturity.

After Wesley decided *The Arminian Magazine* would bear improvement through greater variety, he very soon hit upon the expedient of printing original sermons. He had already published a number of his discourses separately and in collections, and now in volume four of the magazine new ones began to appear. In addition to his own, there was a considerable selection from other preachers; some of these had already been in print, and some, like his, were now for the first time available for reading.

The sermons, after all, were no very startling novelty. Though they dealt with a wide range of topics—moral, spiritual, and doctrinal questions which had no immediate connection with the controverted point of Arminianism—sermons were what might readily have been expected in a religious journal. But Wesley conceived the idea that *The Arminian Magazine* might be used to bring useful information to his Methodists as well as to strengthen them in cardinal principles of theology and religion. The more intelligent a man was and the broader and more cultivated his tastes, the better and more effective Christian he would be—provided only that he never overstepped the sanctions laid down in Scripture. In a multitude of ways Wesley had endeavored for years to introduce to his people some of the riches of his own cultural heritage, and now he turned his magazine to account in his effort "to learn and propagate" his conception of "the best that has been thought and said in the world."

The extent to which he could accomplish such an aim in the magazine was limited by the relatively restricted educational and cultural background of the vast majority of his subscribers. It was his method to keep the intellectual level somewhat above that of the average reader. Sometimes he was aware of having dangled his plums a trifle too high for them to jump after. "It was objected . . . ," he wrote in the preface to the second volume, "that 'some of the tracts are hard to be understood.' I allow that they were; but those that follow will be plainer and plainer; so that I trust they will be easily understood by any one of a tolerable capacity." But he was not long willing that the whole magazine should be held in leash for the slow-witted. He noticed a similar objection in the preface to volume seven: "Perhaps it may be said . . . , 'Some articles . . . , particularly the extracts from Mr. Bryant, and the extracts from and remarks upon Mr. Locke, are not intelligible to common readers.' I know it well; but did I ever say this was intended for common readers only? By no means. I publish it for the sake of the learned as well as the unlearned readers. But as the latter are the greater number, nine parts in ten of the work are generally suited to their capacity. What they do not understand, let them leave to others, and endeavour to profit by what they do understand." This determination of Wesley's sometimes led him to what amounted to an extreme of abstruseness, as when he wrote an argumentative discussion of the orthography of vowel-points in the Hebrew language. But such occasions were quite rare. Ordinarily he pursued a policy of introducing, now and then, an article of universal interest, but of texture sufficiently tough to exercise the teeth of his readers.

The nature of his magazine was changing, and Wesley knew it. In the preface to volume seven he noticed the wording of his title-page: "The Arminian Magazine, consisting of Extracts and Treatises on Universal Redemption." That was no longer a strictly true indication of the contents, for articles bearing specifically on the subject were, as he said, "but a very inconsiderable part of it; seldom above nine or ten pages in a number." In spite of the little space devoted to enforcing doctrine, he persistently asserted the necessity of emphasizing Arminian principles. "Therefore," he announced, "I will order the title-page to run thus for the time to come: '*The Arminian Magazine,* consisting chiefly of Extracts and Treatises on Universal Redemption.'" And it was so.

In the new sections as well as in the old, articles original with other men were many times in excess of those spun from Wesley's own brain. He continued to exercise at large his remarkable proclivity for abridging works already in print; he collected fresh material from divers sources; and, of course, he sat in judgment upon the voluntary contributions which began to flow in upon him.

His original contributions form a curiously heterogeneous miscellany. In publishing sermons he was upon familiar ground. But he struck out in new directions. There were essays whose abstract titles, "Thoughts on Genius," "Thoughts upon Taste," and the like, inevitably suggest that he was venturing the danger of comparison with Francis Bacon. His critical essays were of two not very sharply defined types. Such pieces as his "Thoughts on Jacob Behmen" were little more than thinly veiled bits of controversial divinity; whereas his "Thoughts on the Character and Writings of Mr. Prior" stood quite solidly upon literary grounds—it was about as far from being a religious tract as Johnson's life of the poet. Between these two extremes were other criticisms whose bias was in a greater or less degree literary. Besides such formal, full-length essays as these, there were paragraphs here and there in the magazine into which Wesley would compress a bit of useful or otherwise interesting information which he had picked up. He would tell why dew forms on coach-glasses, correct the current false notion of the character of Epicurus, or give an etymological history of an unusual word.

It had been Wesley's original intention to avoid serial publication: it seemed to him an absurd thing to use such an obvious and irritating bait for subscriptions. But experience taught him that the reader is often caught by what he least likes. He made good use of his changed policy, for it enabled him to print a number of excellent standard treatises too long to be given in one issue. Best known of these was Locke's *Essay on the Human Understanding.* It was a favorite with Wesley. He carefully abridged it, cut it into suitable divisions, and appended notes. These "remarks," as he called them, were sometimes objections to parts of Locke's system, sometimes explanations, and sometimes practical interpretations of abstract ideas.

Wesley's widely eclectic interests enabled him to bring several fields of knowledge to the use of his subscribers. Natural philosophy appeared from several sources, including his own *Survey of the Wisdom of God in the Creation;* recent discoveries in physics and electricity were transferred from Benjamin Franklin and other experimenters; Bryant's *Analysis of Ancient Mythology* brought echoes of the early civilizations, and *An Extract from an Account of the Pelew Islands,* by Captain Henry Wilson, told of strange and hitherto unknown races of men. An account of the new Sunday School movement, a description of the manner in which one might avoid thirsting to death when adrift at sea, and illustrations of the horrible practices of the slave-trade—these and a multitude of other informative articles brought a wealth of new ideas to widen many a family's narrow horizon.

Narratives also began to appear in *The Arminian Magazine.* Most prominent were stories of the supernatural. As Southey would have it, Wesley "indulged his indiscriminate credulity, and inserted, without scruple, and without reflection, any marvelous tale that came to his hands."[12] It is certainly true that an enormous number of such tales found places in the magazine—tales built upon witchcraft, possession by devils, second sight, and all manner of incidents wherein the natural order of events seemed to be disturbed by the interposition of supernatural forces. The interest in distant lands, which was gaining a fresh influence over fiction, brought to *The Arminian Magazine* "A Turkish Tale" and other stories with an exotic flavor. The irrepressible sentimentality of the period dripped a few tears in its pages, only to receive a healthy antidote from an occasional bit of infectious humor.

As one thumbs through the pages of *The Arminian Magazine* today, one finds among its quaint and curious extracts of forgotten lore many a fascinating page. The mean level of excellence in the poetry section is above the need of commendation. In the bulk of the prose the modern reader feels less at home: there is much that has become dull and lifeless, and a little searching is necessary unless one is lucky enough to hit upon a choice morsel at first opening. Nevertheless, a surprisingly large fraction of the whole is still interesting.

For example, there are such amusing pieces as this which follows:[18]

> To be jocular in death is preposterous; nor is it less so to inscribe low jests on the Monuments of the dead. We insert the following as a remarkable instance of this sort of buffoonery, found, in a country Churchyard, on the Tomb-stone of one Katharine Gray, who in her life-time had been a dealer in earthenware.
>
> To understand this ridiculous piece, you are to follow the letters, till they make up a word: not regarding whether they be great or small; nor how they are divided, or pointed.

Bene
AT. HT. his: ST.
Oneli Eska
Thari Neg Rayc
Hang'd
F. R
O! mab. U. Sy li Fet
olif. Ele
s S. *c* L
Ayb. Ye. *ar*
Than
Dcl——Ays
Hego
Therp. Elfa.
n. d

No. *ws*. He Stur
n'dt. oea Rt.
Hh? ersel. Fy,
Ew E—E. Pin
Gfr. I. EN
DS L
etm. EA. D
VI?
Seab AT eyo
URG
Rie. Fan
D D
Ryy O! U—Rey
Esf, OR WH
ATA

Vai——Ls aflo
O! Doft Ears. W.
Hok No WSB
Ut Ina Runo
Fy Ears
In So—Metall
Pit——C

Hero R broa
D P
Ans He I
N H
Ers Hopma
Y B
E AG———AIN

At any rate Wesley's people were delighted, and the magazine grew steadily in popularity. He himself expressed some surprise. He had expected to run it only for a year or so, but the increasing demand encouraged him to continue.[14]

He fostered the growth carefully and intelligently. He required that the articles be entertaining as well as profitable. As early as the first year, he began including pictures—engraved portraits of men in whom Methodist people were interested—and thereafter took great pains to insure their excellence in design and execution. But in spite of the fact that he was sensitive to any indication of popular taste, and in spite of the fact that he was in close touch with more people than any other man in England, and had, therefore, better opportunities of knowing what would be appealing to them, surely he owed some debt to mere good fortune in that he so accurately touched the springs of interest which were flowing then almost flush with the surface. That he capitalized the obvious trends is certain. But he profited from others which were not yet clearly manifest. Partly, no doubt, he had himself been responsible for bringing these elements up from the depths. But that he was aware of their full literary implications is hardly conceivable. If good fortune was his ally, however, he was assisted no less powerfully by the force of his own tremendous prestige. Hampson, the biographer, who, utterly despising *The Arminian Magazine,* could find no other explanation for its popularity, accounted for the wide sale solely as "a remarkable proof of the authority of his name."[15]

Whatever the reason may have been, at the period of Wesley's death the annual circulation had reached 7,000.[16] That is a fairly large number, but it is not an adequate representation of the reading public the journal reached. Among people of the early Methodists' financial standing, a magazine was a precious thing. Personal devotion to Mr. Wesley and an unusual religious zeal made them extraordinarily eager to read; and the closely knit organization and the communal fellowship of the members made borrowing and lending the most natural thing in the world. So the number of readers was actually far greater than the figure mentioned. This success rendered it one of Wesley's most effective instruments of religious and cultural enlightenment.

CHAPTER SIX

JOHN WESLEY AS POET

JOHN WESLEY very early gave evidence that he shared the strain of poetry which ran in his family. A capable student in every department of study, he was particularly distinguished at the Charterhouse for his excellent translations from the Latin. The source of pleasure thus discovered continued during the period of residence at Oxford, finding expression in exercises of translation and paraphrase.

"Mr. Wesley's natural temper in his youth," as Dr. Whitehead said, "was gay and sprightly, with a turn for wit and humor."[1] For instance, an hour or so spent in concocting a poem to send to his convalescent brother brought forth the following choice morsel of ridicule taken "From the Latin:"

As o'er fair *Cloe's* rosy cheek,
  Careless, a little vagrant passed,
With artful hand around his neck
  A slender chain the virgin cast.

As *Juno* near her throne above
  Her spangled bird delights to see,
As *Venus* has her fav'rite dove,
  Cloe shall have her fav'rite flea.

Pleased at his chains, with nimble steps
  He o'er her snowy bosom strayed:
Now on her panting breast he leaps,
  Now hides between his little head.

Leaving at length his old abode,
  He found, by thirst or fortune led,
Her swelling lips, that brighter glowed
  Than roses in their native bed.

Cloe, your artful bands undo,
  Nor for your captive's safety fear;
No artful bands are needful now
  To keep the willing vagrant here.

Whilst on that heav'n 'tis given to stay,
  (Who would not wish to be so blest?)
No force can draw him once away,
  Till Death shall seize his destined breast.

Wesley's comment on his stanzas is terse: "There is one, and I am afraid but one, good thing in them—that is, they are short."[2]

It was from his favorite Horace that Wesley translated most of the early, secular verse which remains to us. One such piece the biographies have prudently and with one accord neglected to notice: the nineteenth ode of Horace's first book. The only fault the youthful future leader of Methodism could find in his verses was their need of careful revision and correction. Here are the last three stanzas:

No more the wand'ring Scythian's might
  From softer themes my lyre shall move;
No more the Parthian's wily flight:
  My lyre shall sing of naught but Love.

Haste, grassy altars let us rear;
  Haste, wreaths of fragrant myrtle twine;
With Arab sweets perfume the air,
  And crown the whole with gen'rous wine.

While we the sacred rites prepare,
  The cruel Queen of fierce desires
Will pierce, propitious to my prayer,
  The obdurate maid with equal fires.[3]

Since, however, Wesley was never thoroughly at home except where his speech could be positive and emphatic on a moral question, Horace's famous "Integer Vitae" gave him material more nearly suited to the decisiveness of his natural temperament. "Integrity needs no defense," he began; and, despite their tautology, the last two stanzas achieve at least something of the resonance and force of his later religious verse:

Place me where no revolving sun
Does e'er his radiant circles run,
Where clouds and damps alone appear
And poison the unwholesome year:

Place me in that effulgent day
Beneath the sun's directer ray;
No change from its fixed place shall move
The basis of my lasting love.[4]

Secular themes were well enough for making profitable an idle hour, but Wesley, even now convinced that the deepest and purest source of human inspiration lay in the Holy Scriptures, based his most ambitious single flight on the first eighteen sonorous verses of the 104th Psalm. His mother saw the result and wisely advised him: "I would not have you leave off making verses; rather make poetry sometimes your diversion, though never your business."[5]

When Wesley was free to expand his text and introduce original elements for poetic ornamentation, he was prone to rely too much on the conventional idioms which were to become the laughing stock of later criticism. The first two stanzas are a fair sample of the whole (if, indeed, they are not easily the best):

Upborne aloft on vent'rous wing
While, spurning earthly themes, I soar,
Through paths untrod before,
What God, what seraph shall I sing?
Whom but thee should I proclaim,
Author of this wond'rous frame?
Eternal, uncreated Lord,
Enshrin'd in glory's radiant blaze!
At whose prolific voice, whose potent word,
Commanded, nothing swift retir'd, and worlds began their race.

Thou, brooding o'er the realms of night,
Th' unbottom'd infinite abyss,
Bad'st the deep her rage surcease,
And said'st let there be light!,
Aethereal light thy call obey'd,
Glad she left her native shade,
Through the wide void her living waters past;
Darkness turn'd his murmuring head,
Resign'd the reins, and trembling fled;
The crystal waves roll'd on, and filled the ambient waste.[6]

Nothing could be said about the poem in its entirety that would be quite so devastating as an acceptance of its implied invitation to comparison with the Psalm. Wesley's miscarriage in this instance is highly significant: he beflowers his original and adds new material for no good purpose except decoration. Fortunately, by the time he came to write the adaptations and translations which were to furnish new blood to English hymnody he had found his proper talent. In his best work he cut away superfluous ornament instead of adding new frills: he condensed and simplified, and when his own words replaced the phrasing of his original, it was always for a better purpose than merely spinning out rhythmical, high-sounding sentences.

Of the foreign hymns Wesley turned into English, by far the most important and numerous are those from the German. His first study of that language was stimulated by the presence, on the ship which bore him to America, of twenty-six Moravians whose religious zeal made him eager for their conversation.[7] Before the *Simmonds* touched the shores of the New World he was at home with them. Not content with a mere speaking knowledge, he spent much time in Georgia systematically and thoroughly performing his self-imposed task: he talked and sang in German; read German books; wrote in German; mastered and reviewed a German grammar and a German dictionary, then transcribed them to fix their contents in his memory; and, finally, he wrote a German grammar and compiled a German dictionary of his own.[8]

From this time until 1740, when he drew his Methodists away from the Fetter Lane Society of Moravians in London, he was almost continuously in contact and communication with German-speaking people. Many important results ensued. He fell heir to the long tradition of German religious devotion which had its well-spring in the days of Martin Luther, and he appropriated for the English language the rich sentiment which that tradition had developed. Not since the days of Miles Coverdale, two centuries before, had this vein been tapped. It was John Wesley who independently recognized the excellence of German hymnody and who effectively stimulated Englishmen's interest in its beauty.[9]

Heretofore the English Church had had nothing which could properly be called a hymn-book. What congregational singing there was depended upon two metrical versions of the Psalms: that containing what Wesley termed "the miserable, scandalous doggerel" of Sternhold and Hopkins, and the New Version by Tate and Brady.[10] But in 1736 in the remote colony of Georgia a busybody young high-church clergyman with a literary conscience was tempering the wedge of a minor revolution. He was collecting hymns which had proved their excellence among the Dissenters, and casting devotional material from several sources into a form that could be sung by congregations. While the collection existed only in his manuscript, the poems underwent the test of use at numerous religious meetings. Those which survived, he polished and tested again. Next year, taking the finished manuscript to Charlestown, South Carolina, he published *A Collection of Psalms and Hymns,* which was the first hymnbook ever prepared for use in the services of the English Established Church.[11]

Here appeared the first few of those pieces he spoke of in later years when, recalling his early contact with the Moravians, he said, "I translated many of their hymns for the use of our own congregations. Indeed, as I durst not implicitly follow any man, I did not take all that lay before me; but selected those which I judged to be most scriptural and most suitable to sound experience."[12]

Not even when he had chosen the hymns to be translated did he "implicitly follow" any author. To be sure, he always shows a highly accurate apprehension of the meaning of his text; so that his divergences from the original cannot be accounted for on the ground of a misreading.[13] But in most cases he freely adapted the German to accord with his own purposes, and rephrased it to suit his own taste and judgment.

When his near agreement with the original permitted a close translation, Wesley was peculiarly fortunate in finding accurate poetic phrases.[14] He was no more able to retain the timbre of foreign verse than any other translator has been, but he supplied in its place a certain forthright manner of his own, quite in keeping with the genius of English poetry.

Statements or implications to which he had definite objections, he calmly omitted. Although some such omissions can be accounted for on the ground that the passages had to do with unacceptable theological attitudes, more frequently his objections proceeded from what is best described as a sense of good taste. It frequently happens that the figurative language of intense religious devotionalism becomes offensive if not indecent. Wesley himself employed that violent Scriptural metaphor of self-abasement so dear to eighteenth century pietism. Quite consistent, however, with his willingness to hear worshippers call themselves worms, was his emphatic denunciation of a familiar or sensuous approach to Diety. His preachers received many a rebuke for bold, irreverent, improper expressions in prayer, especially for the "armorous" manner of supplication.[15] So also in his translations of hymns he avoided following the original into irreverently sensuous imagery. The Germans had carried beyond all bounds of decorum their elaboration of the conception of Christ as the lover or bridegroom of the human soul. According to his own statement, Wesley "particularly endeavoured, in all the hymns which are addressed to our blessed Lord, to avoid every *fondling* expression, and to speak as to the most high God; to him that is 'in glory equal with the Father, in majesty co-eternal.' "[16] Many a kiss and fond embrace failed to appear in his English versions.[17]

"Perhaps some may be afraid," said Wesley, "lest the refraining from these warm expressions, or even gently checking them, should check the fervor of our devotions. It is very possible it may check, or even prevent, some kind of fervor which has passed for devotion. Possibly it may prevent loud shouting, horrid, unnatural screaming, repeating the same words twenty or thirty times, jumping two or three feet high, and throwing about the arms or legs, both of men and women, in a manner shocking not only to religion, but to common decency:—But it will never check, much less prevent, true, scriptural devotion. It will even enliven the prayer that is properly addressed to Him, who, though he was very man, yet was very God: who, though he was born of a woman, to redeem man; yet was God from everlasting, and world without end."[18]

In matters of form Wesley's guiding principles were brevity and simplicity. With but one exception (the stately hymn "High on His Everlasting Throne," from Spangenberg's "Der König ruht, und schauet doch"), the translations are appreciably shorter than the originals.[19] And the German hymns, with their complicated metrical schemes, their acrostics, and their alternation of masculine and feminine rimes, fall into the regular, familiar, masculine patterns of the English hymn tradition.[20]

Wesley packed as much meaning into line and stanza as simplicity and clearness would allow. For example, in Gerhardt's hymn "O Jesu Christ, mein schönstes Licht" there occurs the line

so lauff ich mit den füssen.

Recognizing how absurd a literal rending would sound to English ears, Wesley wrote

So shall I run and never tire,

thereby introducing not only a fresh idea but also an allusion to Scripture.

Love of Milton and the Hebrew poetry gave him a touch of that grand, sweeping majesty which is so rare and excellent a trait in hymn writers. Many seek a majestic tone; but the resulting lines are usually mere sound and fury. Wesley's best claim to poetic honors is based on the fact that what he said of the Methodist hymns as a whole can truly be applied to his own translations: "In these hymns there is no doggerel, no botches, nothing put in to patch up the rhyme, no feeble expletives. Here is nothing turgid or bombastic on the one hand, or low and creeping on the other. Here are no cant expressions, no words without meaning. . . . Here are . . . both the purity, the strength, and the elegance of the English language, and, at the same time, the utmost simplicity and plainness."[21]

It is possible in some measure to indicate the traits which distinguish Wesley's hymns for their grandeur. As Professor Hatfield has pointed out,[22] Wesley was fond of employing balanced phrases that build emphatic climaxes of thought. For example, he translates

> alles was da lebet in dir webet

as

> All things in Earth, and Air, and Sea,
> Exist, and live, and move in Thee.[23]

Sometimes Wesley's lofty tone is the result of a felicitous employment of words which inevitably imply dramatic action or which call striking pictures before the mind's eye.

> Du einiger und wahrer Gott,
> du herrscher aller himmels-scharren

becomes

> Thou, true and only God, lead'st forth
> Th' immortal Armies of the Sky.

A forceful verb may give power to a line, as when

> Dass er die Seelen drum verliert
> Und sie der Heiland mit sich führt

is rendered

> To tear the Prey out of Thy Teeth;
> To spoil the Realms of Hell and Death.[24]

Wesley translated only one German hymn after his separation from the Moravians; by 1743 his work of this kind was done. But he had accomplished a good deal. English hymnody was left with a number of poems which are intrinsically at least as excellent as their distinguished German originals; he had opened a field which, by the end of the next century, had yielded a large and splendid body of translated sacred poetry to English-speaking congregations; and he had widened and deepened a channel which was to have a great, if not altogether measurable effect upon the whole range of English poetry.

Wesley's translations of the German hymns constitute what is permanent in his poetic work. Of a more exclusively historic importance, but no less indicative of a desire to supply the devotional needs of his congregation with as much good poetry as he could find, was his series of adaptations from George Herbert's religious verse.

In preparing an effective body of such literature for his parishoners he was at the same time laboring to meet hs own wants. During the sojourn in Georgia, whither he had gone for the express purpose of saving his own soul, the young clergyman yet lacked that personal assurance of the presence of God which he expected would be his salvation. Consequently, George Herbert, who, as Richard Baxter remarked,[25] "speaks to God like one that really believeth a God, and whose business in this world is most with God," appealed to him with peculiar force. Izaak Walton[26] had called *The Temple* "a book, by the frequent reading whereof, and the assistance of that spirit that seemed to inspire the author, the reader may attain habits of peace and piety, and all the gifts of the Holy Ghost and heaven, and may by still reading still keep those sacred fires burning upon the altar of so pure a heart, as shall free it from the anxieties of the world, and keep it fixed upon things that are above." Such a consummation was devoutly to be wished.

Perhaps communal meditation upon the thoughts of the poet would be even more effectual than solitary reading. So he began that study which is traceable in the Savannah diaries through the frequent mention of "Herbert". Wesley was selecting short pieces from *The Temple* and re-versifying them for congregational singing. A few specimens of his work appeared in the Charlestown *Collection of Psalms and Hymns,* but his love for Herbert continued until in subsequent editions of hymnals the number of paraphrases from this source reached forty-two.[27]

A comparison of the new versions with Herbert's poems shows that Wesley followed a procedure in many respects similar to his treatment of the German hymns.

First of all, he recast Herbert's irregular lines of various lengths into more normal stanzas. When the original adhered to a sufficiently simple metrical design, as was the case with "The Elixir", he accepted its form; but Herbert's fondness for variety, expressing itself frequently for example, by a shift from eight syllables to four per line within a stanza, usually rendered a change necessary. Wesley's favorite verse was the tetrameter, with the trimeter running a not too distant second. He apparently felt that dimeter and pentameter lines did not suit the genius of the hymn-tune, for he consistently avoided them.

Simplicity and complete clarity of meaning were necessary if the poems were to be useful outside the leisurely, thoughtful atmosphere of the study. Accordingly, the slight obscurity of this stanza from "The Elixir",

All may of thee partake:
Nothing can be so mean,
Which with his tincture (*for thy sake*)
Will not grow bright and clean,

disappears when Wesley interprets the meaning and renders the corresponding stanza:

All may of Thee partake:
Nothing so small can be,
But draws, when acted for Thy sake,
Greatness and worth from Thee.

For a like reason, the "metaphysical" conceits, with their tendency to make the reader pause and reflect upon the full import of passing allusions, were hardly consonant with the primarily emotional impact of congregational singing. Herbert writes, in his exquisite "Virtue",

Only a sweet and virtuous soul,
Like seasoned timber, never gives;
But though the whole world turn to coal,
Then chiefly lives.

Figurative language is just as much an acceptable part of hymns as it is of other types of poetry. But if the singer's attention is to be kept centered in the dominant theme, and if his emotional response is to be prevented from dissipating itself in the intellectual pursuit of an auxiliary idea, the figures must immediately present the full content of their meaning, an end only to be achieved through the use of either familiar or very general terms. Hence, when Wesley adapted the stanza from "Virtue" he wrote:

Only a sweet and virtuous mind,
When Nature all in ruin lies,
When earth and heaven a period find,
Begins a life that never dies.

The same principles find illustration in the two versions of "Vanity". In the original the third stanza runs thus:

The subtle Chymic can divest
And strip the creature naked, till he find
The callow principles within their nest;
There he imparts to them his mind,
Admitted to their bedchamber, before
They appear trim and drest
To ordinary suitors at the door.

By conventionalization Wesley not only avoided calling the mind to dwell on the implications of a metaphysical conceit, but unprudishly eliminated the slightest hint of sensuality from the image:

The subtle Chemist can divest
Gay Nature of her various hue;
Stript of her thousand forms, confest
She stands, and naked to his view;
At distance other suitors stand;
Her inmost stores wait his command.

This stanza from "Vanity" also exemplifies another invariable practice of Wesley's. Archaic words he modernized, as he did "Chymic"; and hard or unusual words, like "callow", he either displaced with easy ones or evaded in some other way.

Wesley was meticulously careful lest any production of his, whether translation or adaptation, contain the merest shadow of irreverence to God. Thus, when he was paraphrasing "The Reprisal" he omitted an entire stanza for no other apparent reason than that in the original it implied the possibility of a sort of equality between man on the one hand and Christ as God on the other:

Ah! was it not enough that thou
By thy eternal glory didst outgo me?
Could'st thou not grief's sad conquest me allow,
But in all victories overthrow me?

There are further differences between Herbert's verse and Wesley's which cannot be fully exemplified by a few stanzas. To an appreciable degree, Wesley was influenced by the poetic fashions of which Pope and Watts, respectively, stand as leaders. But much of what is new in his paraphrases proceeded from elements which had become so thoroughly assimilated as to be characteristically his own.

Whereas Herbert, in common with other poets of the metaphysical school, consciously shunned loftiness of metrical tone, Wesley's verse possesses a resonance and an exulting strength which may be supposed to have a sort of appropriateness to his conception of God's majesty. This trait is partially susceptible of analysis: we can notice Wesley's unhesitating use of the superlative (as in "Her inmost stores"), and terms which are beyond the need of the superlative (such as "a life that never dies"); but in general we may content ourselves with observing that his poetic style is in accord with his own personality. It is emphatic, reverent, inclined to action rather than reflection, and shot through with a sense of the overpowering greatness of God.

The adaptations from George Herbert were not so permanently successful as the translations from the German. The test of time has proved them ill adapted to congregational singing. Perhaps the principal reason for their unpopularity lies in the fact that by their very nature the poems were incapable of being wrought into instruments of that predominantly emotional, almost dramatic appeal which the really great hymn exercises. They were not written as songs; their thoughts required too many lines to come to a comprehensible point. And in spite of Wesley's skill in producing versions whose meter would technically fit a tune, the singing quality simply did not exist in them.

It is hard to tell whether even during Wesley's lifetime these poems were often sung in Methodist meetings. It is possible, of course, that the momentum of the revival carried them along, caught in the surge and flow of Watts' and Charles Wesley's ecstatic voices. But it seems much more probable that in public services they gave way to other hymns: that they were reserved for solitary use in private devotions. Most of the Wesleyan hymnbooks of the eighteenth century were simply books of religious poems, without musical notation. They served the same purposes as any other book of religious verse, except that they had an additional value because of their capacity for guiding congregational singing. Not all the hymns of even Charles Wesley were expected to be sung; doubtless many that he wrote as well as a large fraction of those by other men which were printed along with his in *The Arminian Magazine* were never so much as fitted to a tune. The adaptations from Herbert, therefore, could have been, and it seems reasonable to believe that they actually were, eventually relegated to the single function of providing poetry for the Methodists.

Besides the translations from the German and the adaptations from George Herbert, which were undoubtedly John Wesley's, there were three contributions to the Methodist hymnal which can be attributed to him with a confidence only just short of certainty. One was a paraphrase of the Lord's Prayer in three parts; one was a translation from an unknown Spanish author, the hymn beginning "O God, my God, my all thou art;" and one was a translation from a hymn by the French mystic, Madame Bourignon: "Come, Saviour, Jesus, from above."

* * * * * * *

If one may judge from the diary entries made while he was in Georgia, John Wesley composed there some verse which was strictly original. But inasmuch as the Wesley hymns were usually published conjointly under the names of Charles and John, without any notation to indicate specifically the authors of the separate poems, we are at a loss to separate the work of the one from that of the other.[28] Unless some as yet undiscovered evidence is brought to light, we must refrain from ascribing to John Wesley any of the poetry except pieces such as those we have been reviewing, which can be definitely proved to have been his.[29]

With one exception, all the verse we know Wesley wrote after he left Oxford to take up the work of the Christian ministry was designed to be used in religious worship. The exception was the result of a major emotional crisis in his life. When Grace Murray, whom he loved, had broken her engagement with him in favor of one John Bennett, he was more profoundly stirred than he would permit his outward appearance to indicate. One day in 1749, while riding from Leeds to Newcastle, he gave vent to his feelings in the matter by drawing up "A short Account of the whole" in verse.[30]

Characteristically, he began by appealing to God:

O Lord, I bow my sinful Head!
  Righteous are all thy ways with Man!
Yet suffer me with Thee to plead,
  With lowly reverence to complain;
With deep, unutter'd Grief to groan,
O what is this that Thou hast done!

After a short review of his own early experiences of love, he entered into a narration of Grace Murray's career, beginning with her childhood.

In early Dawn of Life, Serene,
  Mild, sweet, and tender was her Mood:
Her pleasing Form spoke all within
  Soft and compassionately good:
Listening to every Wretch's Care,
Mixing with each her friendly Tear.

At Dawn of Life, to feed the Poor
  Glad she her little All bestow'd:
Wise to lay up a better Store,
  And hast'ning to be rich in God;
God whom she sought with early Care,
With reverence and with lowly Fear.

The narration continued through the betrothal. Recalling his happiness in the knowledge of her love, Wesley thought again of her vows:

Oft (tho' as yet the Nuptial Tie
  Was not), clasping her Hand in mine,
What Force, she said, beneath the Sky,
  Can now our well-knit Souls disjoin?
With Thee I'd go to India's Coast,
To Worlds in distant Ocean lost!

The blow fell, and Wesley turned again to God, who, he trusted, was agent in all these things, with a prayer in which he achieves for once the heights of true poetry.

What Thou hast done I know not now!
  Suffice I shall hereafter know!
Beneath Thy chastening Hand I bow:
  That still I live to Thee I owe.
O teach Thy deeply-humbled Son
To say, "Father, thy Will be done!"

Teach me, from every pleasing Snare
  To keep the Issues of my Heart:
Be Thou my Love, my Joy, my Fear!
  Thou my eternal Portion art.
Be Thou my never-failing Friend,
And love, O love me to the End!

At Oxford Wesley had followed Horace in the vow, "My lyre shall sing of naught but Love." But somehow "The cruel Queen of fierce desires" had failed to pierce "The obdurate maid with equal fires" in every instance wherein this was Wesley's prayer. It is a significant fact that on the only occasion we can be sure he was playing on a lyre of his own, Wesley ended by singing the real master passion of his life, the divine love of God.

CHAPTER SEVEN

METHODIST HYMNS

EVEN THOUGH we follow the traditional practice in ascribing all the original Wesley hymns to Charles, we cannot evade the fact that John Wesley to a marked degree shares the credit for their position at the forefront of Christian devotional poetry.

Charles, to be sure, was the one man to whose taste and judgment his brother deferred. Editing *The Arminian Magazine* devolved entirely upon John Wesley except in the department containing poetry. There, he said, "Only my brother and I are the judges what pieces shall be admitted."[1] Furthermore, he could not quite bring himself to denounce, in Charles' hymn, a "glowing expression" which, had it occurred in any other man's poetry, would have provoked his wrath.[2]

And yet inevitably Charles Wesley's hymns felt John's restraining and guiding hand. By nature Charles was akin to the German devotional writers; he had that poetic susceptibility to sense-impressions which, joined with a mystic consciousness of God's immanence, tended to resolve all religious emotion into luxurious rapture. The counterbalancing force which prevented his words from running to unwarrantable lengths was the influence of his sympathetic but more literal-minded brother.

Some volumes of Charles Wesley's hymns went through the press without being subjected to John's revision. Speaking of the two volumes of *Hymns and Sacred Poems* printed in 1749, the latter protested: "As I did not see these before they were published, there were some things in them which I did not approve of."[3] But ordinarily, and particularly in the collections of hymns recommended for use in congregations, John Wesley exercised the editorial prerogative only less rigorously over Charles' hymns than over others.

A glance at those he excluded reveals not only his aversion to overbold imagery and unsound doctrine, but also his usual sense of artistic decorum. Charles was an experimenter in metrical design; his wide variety of stanza forms stood together with Herbert's verse in sharp contrast with John's strictly limited range. The latter, adhering to simplicity on principle rather than because of any incapacity for variation,[4] consistently chose hymns in familiar measures and rejected those in such eccentric dress as this:

O how sweet it is to languish
For our God
Till his blood
Eases all our anguish.[5]

Even the pieces he saw fit to popularize underwent careful scrutiny and often passed from his hands with many a verbal alteration.

If his dominating will operated to such an extent upon the work of his brother, it goes without saying that John Wesley exercised absolute authority over every word of whatever else appeared in his collections. Though no one will seriously deny to Charles the honorable distinction accorded in his frequent unofficial title as poet-laureate of the Methodist revival, it was John Wesley who really governed the Methodist use of song. "He planned it," declares Louis F. Benson, "prepared the ground, introduced and fostered it, moulded and administered it, and also restrained its excesses."[6]

He was fully conscious of the fact that his task as editor was one to which should be brought great delicacy of taste and soundness of judgment. Observing the desolation wrought by other men, he entered a strong protest: "Many gentlemen have done my Brother and me (though without naming us) the honour to reprint many of our hymns. Now they are perfectly welcome to do so, provided they print them just as they are. But I desire they would not attempt to mend them; for they really are not able. None of them is able to mend either the sense or the verse. Therefore I must beg of them one of these two favours; either to let them stand as they are, to take them for better for worse, or to add the true reading in the margin, or at the bottom of the page; that we may no longer be accountable for the nonsense or for the doggerel of other men."[7]

Observation of the botches made by inexpert hymn tinkerers, however, in no degree diminished Wesley's confidence in his own ability to improve other people's hymns. The remarkable truth is, he was frequently justified even when he laid hands on the work of first-rate hymn-writers. For example, his re-creation of Watts' lines,

> Nations, attend before his throne
> With solemn fear, with sacred joy,

into the more impressively phrased,

> Before Jehovah's awful throne,
> Ye nations, bow with sacred joy,

has found general acceptance in subsequent hymnals of all denominations.[8]

Aware of the psychological effectiveness of the congregational hymn, Wesley performed his editorial function with a definite purpose which he partially stated in the preface to his historic collection of 1780. Its contents were able to demonstrate, he said, "all the important truths of our most holy religion, whether speculative or practical; yea, to illustrate them all, and to prove them both by Scripture and reason. And this is done in a regular order. The hymns are not carelessly jumbled together, but carefully ranged under proper heads, according to the experience of real Christians. So that this book is, in effect, a little body of experimental and practical divinity."[9]

In their intellectual content the hymns carried, as it were, the catechism of Methodist doctrine. Significantly, only one hymn out of the several hundred deals with the terrors of Hell; the vast majority are exuberantly joyful, with the joy either of conscious redemption or of active striving after a spiritual goal. In the hymns, therefore, the intellectual bias and the emotional tone of the revival met and fused into a harmonious unity. Arminianism, as taught by Wesley, was entirely hopeful and hence predominantly happy; even the hymns dealing with death and judgment were songs of triumph or contentment. The penitential hymns, with their plaintive wistfulness, approached the joyful mood from a different direction, but the end of penitence itself was hope.

The hymn book bears witness to a characteristic manifestation of the Methodists' religion. The very act of singing together, of declaring their faith in unison and coupling therewith the indefinable but universal satisfaction of rhythmical, musical sound, was calculated to increase the emotions which prompted them to sing. Hence came the fulfillment of another of Wesley's express purposes: that the hymn book should be for the religious man, "a means of raising or quickening the spirit of devotion, of confirming his faith, of enlivening his hope, and of kindling or increasing his love to God and man."[10]

It is but fitting that this, Wesley's editorial masterpiece, should have been one of the first of his productions to win unstinted praise from men outside the Methodist connection. In 1860 Dr. James Martineau, the distinguished Unitarian wrote: "After the Scriptures, the Wesley Hymn Book appears to me the grandest instrument of popular religious culture that Christendom has ever produced."[11]

This is an extreme statement, but it is significant of a fact Wesley was aware of and considered highly important: that the hymn has power to draw into sympathy and comradeship the divers branches of Protestantism. In 1753, at a time when it was being suggested that the Methodist Societies might some day form a dissenting sect, and when Wesley was beginning his long-continued protest against separation from the Church of England, he published *Hymns and Spiritual Songs, Intended for the Use of Real Christians of all Denominations.* In a preface lamenting "the innumerable mischiefs which have arisen from bigotry," he says: "When will all who sincerely fear God, employ their zeal, not upon ceremonies and notions, but upon justice, mercy, and the love of God! The ease and happiness that attend, the unspeakable advantages that flow from a truly catholic spirit, a spirit of universal love (which is the very reverse of bigotry) one would imagine, might recommend this amiable temper to every person of cool reflection. . . . It is hoped, the ensuing collection of hymns may in some measure contribute . . . to advance this glorious end. . . . There is not an hymn, not one verse inserted here but . . . what every serious and unprejudiced Christian, of whatever denomination, may join in. . . . All these may find herein either such prayers, as speak the language of their souls when they are in heaviness; or such thanksgivings as express, in a low degree, what they feel, when rejoicing with joy unspeakable."[12]

This function of the hymn, in furnishing a common ground for men of conflicting opinions, is almost amusingly illustrated in the reciprocation between the Wesleys and their implacable enemy in the Calvinist camp, Augustus M. Toplady. Toplady was one of the extremely few men whose hymns show the direct influence of Charles Wesley's characteristic manner;[13] and John Wesley exemplified his own teaching by including Toplady's "Rock of Ages" in his hymnal, thereby contributing materially to its great popularity.

The occurrence of John Wesley's name in the index to musical composers in certain modern hymn-books, though it is a merited tribute to his versatility, is likely to mislead some. He deserves recognition for his contribution to church music, not on account of any original work (he actually composed not a single tune of which we have the slightest hint of a record), but because of his activity in popularizing other men's music, in stimulating musical composition for religious purposes, in editing tune-books, in gathering and standardizing a few popular tunes, and in governing the style of singing which made Methodist congregations famous.[14]

He drew upon German music as well as German poetry. Even during the Georgia days he busied himself in fitting together English words and German tunes; and German music was in his mind when, after returning to England and establishing his independent society at the Foundery, he set about preparing a tune-book for use in his meetings.

In 1742 appeared *A Collection of Tunes set to Music, as they are Commonly Sung at the Foundery.* This curious little book contained forty-two tunes with unharmonized melody notation. Interlined with each piece was a hymn-stanza identified by reference to the appropriate page number in *Hymns and Sacred Poems.*[15] Wretched printing rendered it unfit for carrying out Wesley's purposes, but the book is historically interesting for its record of early Methodist music. Fourteen, exactly one-third of the total number, were tunes Wesley had learned from his German friends.[16]

In 1746 was published *Hymns on the Great Festivals,* a selection from several previous volumes of occasional hymns. Interleaved with the twenty-four poems was an equal number of tunes. The music originated under peculiar circumstances. One John

F. Lampe, bassoon player at the Covent Garden Theatre, enjoyed some reputation as a writer on music and as composer of burlesque and comic opera. Under the influence of the Wesleys he underwent conversion and decided, as the phrase goes, to "give up all for Christ." When John Wesley heard of the situation, he commissioned Lampe to compose hymn tunes.[17] The results, part of which comprised the two dozen pieces in *Hymns on the Great Festivals,* were quite popular, and continued for some years in use among the Methodists. However, their entire subjection to an ephemeral musical fashion, their essentially trivial quality, and the limited range of serviceability consequent upon their being written specifically for some of Charles Wesley's more peculiar meters destined them to an unregretted oblivion.[18]

Even contemporaneously, the volume containing Lampe's tunes was useful only under rather narrowly restricted circumstances. Meanwhile, the stock of Methodist tunes was constantly increasing; and as some of the best of these stood in danger of being displaced and then forgotten, a book was sorely needed which should preserve the best and bring them into more common usage throughout the connection. To the *Harmonia Sacra* (c. 1753), a collection of tunes published by his friend Thomas Butts, Wesley gave his hearty commendation.[19] "But this," he said, "though it is excellent in its kind, is not the thing which I want. I want the people called Methodists to sing true the tunes which are in common use among them. At the same time, I want them to have in one volume the best hymns which we have printed; and that in a small and portable volume, and one of an easy price."[20]

He set about satisfying this want, and in 1761 appeared a now quaint-looking forerunner of the modern hymn-and-tune book. It was a double volume entitled *Select Hymns: With Tunes annexed: Designed Chiefly for the use of the People called Methodists.* The first part is devoted to a selection of hymns. The second part contains the music: it has its own pagination, and is fronted by a new title-page, *Sacred Melody: or A Choice Collection of Psalm and Hymn Tunes, with a Short Introduction.* The achievement of this publication cost Wesley some pains. "I have been endeavouring for more than twenty years," he said, "to procure such a book as this; but in vain. Masters of music were above following any direction but their own. And I was determined, whoever compiled this, should follow my direction; not mending our tunes, but setting them down, neither better nor worse than they were. At length I have prevailed. The following collection contains all the tunes which are in common use among us. They are pricked true, exactly as I desire all our congregations may sing them; and here is prefixed to them a collection of those hymns which are, I think, some of the best we have published."[21]

The arrangement of *Sacred Melody* was similar to that of the old "Foundery Collection": one stanza of a hymn was interlined with the unharmonized melody; for the rest of the words one had to turn to the indicated page in the first part of the volume.

The musical notation, in marked contrast with that of the 1742 fiasco, was so far "pricked true" as to enable Wesley to set an exact standard for Methodist song. Determined that the congregations as well as the engraver should follow his direction, he issued authoritative orders: "I. Learn *these tunes* before you learn any others; afterwards learn as many as you please. II. Sing them exactly as they are printed here, without altering or mending them at all; and if you have learned them otherwise, unlearn it as soon as you can."[22]

The "Short Introduction" to *Sacred Melody* is a treatise designed to assist the Methodist people to "sing a tune by the notes." The instructions in the first edition were replaced in subsequent editions by Wesley's better-known essay, *The Grounds of Vocal Music.*[23] Wesley appears not altogether at home in the rôle of music-master; but he went into his task with customary vigor. His terse, picturesque language is sometimes amusing. In giving definitions he makes such statements as: "A *Dot* after a note makes it sound half as long again," and "A *Tril* is the shaking of two distinct notes easily upon one syllable as long as the time allows." And yet he quite well succeeded in his design of explaining musical terms in such a fashion as to be readily understood by the average literate member of his societies.

In addition to providing directions and vocal exercises whereby people might learn to "sing a tune by the notes," he gave instructions for the various practices incidental to congregational singing. For example, he tells how a leader should conduct the group:

> To *beat time,* in slow Common time at the first stroke of the Pendulum strike your hand down; at the second move it to the right, at the third lift it up, at the fourth move it to the left. Or (which is more common) sing the first two notes (or first half) of the Bar, with the hand down, and the last half with it up.
>
> In beating *Triple Time,* the first two thirds of the Bar are usually sung with the hand down; and the last third part of it with the hand up: always observing that the hand must be put down, at the beginning of every perfect Bar; both in Common and Triple Time.

To one who has seen a preacher "hoisting the tune" in a rural chapel, that will call up a vivid memory.

After the volume containing *Sacred Melody* had gone through several editions, Wesley brought out *Sacred Harmony: or a Choice Collection of Psalms and Hymns. Set to Music in two and three parts, for the Voice, Harpsichord and Organ.*[24] This carefully engraved, rather handsome book set the practice which has generally been followed in Methodist and other hymnals: one stanza of the hymn is interlined with the tune, while the remaining stanzas follow in the normal fashion of poetry. However, there is one feature of the book which, though commendable, is now seldom employed: the same tune does not occur twice; after each tune are printed all the hymns intended to be sung to its music.

Sacred Melody and *Sacred Harmony* reveal most of the sources whence the Methodists derived their music. The Psalm tunes of the sixteenth and seventeenth centuries were the foundation: they had been used in the meetings of the old Oxford Holy Club, and they continued to be the basis and strength of the whole body of song. Thomas Tallis, William Birde, Farrant, Este and Ravenscroft, Henry Purcell, and Dr. Croft had found and deepened the main currents in the English hymn tradition. In addition to the innovations of Lampe's temporarily popular music and the enduring strains from Germany, the Wesleys brought in fresh blood from secular sources. Folk music was wrenched away from its traditional function and fitted to religious verse;[25] in fact, any good tune the Wesleys heard, however high or low its origin, stood a chance of being turned to good account with a hymn.

According to a not unlikely story, Charles Wesley once induced a group of rollicking sailors to sing a hymn by composing words to fit the music-hall tune "Nancy Dawson."[26] In sharp contrast stood the strong, chaste music of George Frederick Handel. Handel involuntarily contributed many melodies to the Methodist hymnal through adaptations of themes in his oratorios;[27] but at least three of Charles Wesley's hymns he deliberately set to music.[28]

Urged on by his profound conviction that hymn-singing is a potent means of extending the influence of religion, John Wesley did not rest content with providing words and music for his people; he had definite ideas on proper musical performance, and insisted upon having them practised.

His "Directions for Congregational Singing" subjoined to *Sacred Melody* are gems of common sense couched in crisp language. "Sing *modestly,*" he commanded. "Do not baul, so as to be heard above, or distinct from, the rest of the congregation . . . but strive to unite your voices together, so as to make one clear melodious sound. Sing *in time*. Whatever time is sung, be sure to keep with it. . . . Attend closely to the leading voices, and move therewith as exactly as you can: and take care you sing not too slow. This drawling naturally steals on all who are lazy; and it is high time to drive it out from among us, and sing all our tunes just as quick as we did at first. Above all, sing *spiritually*. Have an eye to God in every word you sing. Aim at pleasing him more than yourself, or any other creature. In order to do this, attend strictly to the sense of what you sing; and see that your heart is not carried away with the sound, but offered to God continually."[29]

The importance of having the attention fixed on the sense of the hymns outweighed all other considerations. After careful scrutiny and revision he insisted that in the Methodist hymns there were, "no cant expressions, no words without meaning. Those who impute this to us know not what they say. We talk common sense, whether they understand it or not, both in verse and prose, and use no word but in a fixed and determinate sense."[30] He was, therefore, determined that those who sang should apprehend the significance of their words. Preachers received instructions to stop short in the midst of a stanza, if the service seemed in danger of dropping into mechanical routine, and ask the people, "Now, do you know what you said last? Did you speak no more than you felt? Did you sing it as unto the Lord, with the spirit and with the understanding also?"[31]

This was a dangerous cure for apathy; and ordinarily Wesley recommended a continuous flow of sound and meaning. The ideal hymn carried an uninterrupted current of thought; and artificial impediment, such as arose out of florid musical scores, received his condemnation. "Beware of *formality* in singing," he told the Conference of 1768, "or it will creep in upon us unawares. Is it not creeping in already, by those complex tunes which it is scarce possible to sing with devotion? Such is 'Praise the Lord, ye blessed ones!' Such the long quavering Hallelujah, annexed to the Morning Song tune, which I defy any man living to sing devoutly. The repeating the same word so often, especially while another repeats different words, shocks all common sense, brings in dead formality and has no more religion in it than a Lancashire hornpipe."[32] That Wesley was not always successful in eliminating real absurdities may be seen from the hymn in *Sacred Melody* which called forth from Wiseman the hurt complaint: "Oh, venerable founder! how could you allow in print

'Grateful unceas
Grateful unceasing sacrifice'?"[33]

But Wesley was struggling against a strong fashion.

For the same reason he opposed florid singing, he deprecated the distractions of counterpoint. Having learned that harmony, in the present accepted sense of the word, was a comparatively recent innovation,[34] he was more than ever firm in his preference for hearing the unison of all voices upon the melody. In commending an exhibition of "such singing as I have seldom heard in England," for example, his specific praise was reserved for the fact that "The women, in particular, sang so exactly that it seemed but one voice."[35]

By every available means, in his letters, in his *Journal Extracts,* in the discussions of the annual conference, in *The Arminian Magazine,* in sermons, and elsewhere he more or less effectively enforced his beliefs about how singing should be performed by congregations. He was the guiding and governing force that made the Methodist hymn a magnet for the multitude and an efficient instrument for the stimulation of profound religious emotion.

CHAPTER EIGHT

THE EDITOR OF POEMS

ON THE FREQUENT OCCASIONS when he answered requests for a course or reading, Wesley almost invariably included a good deal of poetry.[1] He believed in poetry not only as a source of entertainment and aesthetic pleasure, but also as an educative, cultural force, a force which would, under proper circumstances, serve as an ally of Christian doctrine. The most obvious point of contact between poetry and religion was the hymn. But the hymn was a highly specialized form, incapable of variation beyond certain definite limits; and though it was the medium whose possibilities it was Wesley's special service to reveal and exploit, he believed Christian people should have an interest in the wider world of poetry. With characteristic practical energy he proceeded personally to supply the means whereby it might be developed.

The sense of a difference between right and wrong was so fundamental in his nature as not to require statement: it was the axiom of axioms. Sitting in judgment over all social influences, this sense held poetry in its jurisdiction; for poetry was a force which could be exercised in either direction. Standing as an inheritor of the greatest legacies of English poetry, Wesley found that this instrument, "which might answer the noblest purposes, has been prostituted to the vilest, even to confound the distinctions between virtue and vice, good and evil; and that to such a degree that, among the numerous poems now extant in our language, there is an exceedingly small proportion which does not more or less fall under this heavy censure."[2]

There were, he believed, people who agreed with his judgment and others, less willing to put their innocence or virtue to the hazard of exposure to the evil, who were at the same time unwilling "to be deprived of an elegant amusement." He believed, therefore, that many would agree with him in placing "a chaste collection of English poems among the chief desiderata of [the] age."[3]

Accordingly, he reviewed all the English poems he knew, selected what appeared most valuable in them (except that he omitted Spenser "because scarce intelligible to the generality of modern readers"), and, in 1744, published *A Collection of Moral and Sacred Poems. From the most celebrated English Authors,* in three duodecimo volumes.

He praised his anthology in not very alluring terms: "this at least may be affirmed,—there is nothing therein contrary to virtue, nothing that can any way offend the chastest ear, or give pain to the tenderest heart. And perhaps whatever is really essential to the most sublime divinity, as well as the purest and most refined morality, will be found therein. Nor is it a small circumstance that the most just and important sentiments are here represented with the utmost advantage, with all the ornaments both of wit and language, and in the clearest, fullest, strongest light."[4]

Wesley, of course, was perfectly sincere in emphasizing the didactic value of the poems; but there are grounds for believing that he was also employing the highly pietistic flavor of his title and preface as an inducement which should bring people to read first-rate poetry for its own sake. It was his fate to stimulate the conversion of people who tended to express their religious zeal in a sort of intellectual asceticism quite foreign to his nature and quite inconsistent with his conception of the well-rounded Christian life. Overcoming Puritanical narrowness without destroying the foundations of approved moral firmness was a delicate task, but it was one Wesley readily assumed. For your true earnest pietist, the most effective possible recommendation is a statement of a book's religious import. It would be gross falsehood to accuse Wesley of deliberate disingenuousness. The poems are, as a matter of fact, either moral or sacred or both; there was nothing in them that would have offended even a slightly liberal Victorian; and indeed, as he said, "perhaps whatever is really essential to the most sublime divinity, as well as the purest and most refined morality, will be found therein." But "morality", "divinity", and the other commendatory terms must be understood in a broader sense than is usually meant by one who glibly uses them.

Allowing for the inclusion of a very few authors for personal reasons,[5] one whose interests are literary rather than primarily religious would feel called upon to offer no apology for the contents of the volumes. Milton, Dryden, and Pope supplied generous sections; and the pieces from Cowley, Congreve, Prior, Parnell, and Dyer reveal an editorial discretion usually at one with the winnowing of that ultimate critic, time. The numerous selections from Latin poetry, printed in translation, showed excellent taste. Even the distinctively religious verse, which included the works of such men as George Herbert, Roscommon, Norris, Watts, and Edward Young, reveals a mind sensitive as well to poetic value as to sincere devotional fervor.

In some cases, Wesley was evidently drawn two ways by his admiration of a poem and his desire to avoid seeming to recommend what was contrary to his own beliefs. He included the whole of Pope's *Essay on Man,* but was far from being deceived into thinking its teachings consonant with religion. By way of warning the reader against blind acceptance of Pope's dogmatic utterances, he wrote brief footnotes which chime queerly with the polished lines of the text. He begins by commenting upon the prefactory advertisement that the poem contains an ethical structure: "I believe this is as perfect as system of ethics as can well be form'd independent of the Christian System." To Pope's doleful plaint,

> Man never is, but always to be blest,

he replies, "Yes, Blessed is the man whose iniquity is forgiven, and his sin cover'd." An illuminating commentary on Wesley's nature and on the tenacity with which he clung to his chosen touchstone of truth was evoked by the couplet,

> Self-love but serves the virtuous Mind to wake,
> As the small Pebble stirs the peaceful Lake.

"A fine thought!" exclaims the editor. "But is it consistent with Scripture? I am afraid not."

The *Collection of Moral and Sacred Poems* is such a work as could be executed only by a man of broad, liberal culture, whose extensive reading had reinforced a sound, independent critical judgment. That many of the poems should reflect the neo-classical ideal was inevitable and right; but the space given to Milton, to the metaphysical poets, and to early "precursors of romanticism" shows that the editor was unwilling to let the prevailing school of criticism silence any meritorious poetic voice. In regard to manner of expression, then, his taste was catholic. In regard to matter, his guiding principle was a preference for a high moral seriousness which, though not inconsistent with an occasional touch of humor, demanded that the poet believe in the worthwhileness of life and be earnestly concerned for man's living it upon a lofty ethical plane.

By an ironic circumstance, the *Moral and Sacred Poems* transgressed the laws of copyright whereby authors and publishers were beginning to secure to themselves the profits arising from literary production. Robert Dodsley called on Wesley and informed him of the piracy. Wesley immediately made the necessary reparation. His letter to Dodsley records the transaction: "Having inadvertently printed in a collection of poems, 3 vols. 12mo., the *Night Thoughts* of Dr. Young, together with some pieces of Mrs. Rowe's, the property of Mr. Robert Dodsley, and having made satisfaction for the same by payment of a £20 Bank Note, and a cheque for £30, payable in three months, I hereby promise not to print the same again in any form whatever."[6] The *Moral and Sacred Poems,* therefore, did not go to a second edition.[7]

Of all poets, Wesley's most constant favorite was John Milton. He stood prominently among the authors read and reread at Oxford, and took his place with Horace, Juvenal, Homer, Shakespeare, and Spenser as one whose work was deemed worthy of careful annotation.[8] When the endless journeys of the itinerary had made it clear that if Wesley was to have a permanent private library it must exist at least in triplicate at London, Bristol, and Newcastle, Milton, along with Spenser, supplied the irreducible minimum of English poetry.[9] In 1763 he believed it true that "Of all the poems which have hitherto appeared in the world, in whatever age or nation, the preference has generally been given, by impartial judges, to Milton's 'Paradise Lost' ";[10] and with judges who were thus impartial he heartily agreed.

Recognition of such great worth impelled Wesley to desire that it be made available to the people over whose reading he exercised some control. "But," he said, "this inimitable work, amidst all its beauties, is unintelligible to abundance of readers: the immense learning which he has everywhere crowded together, making it quite obscure to persons of common education."[11] He had despaired of putting his other greatly beloved poem, *The Faerie Queene,* into a form which would preserve any of its pristine splendor and at the same time be comprehensible to the multitude. The barrier Milton had raised, though by nature different, was just as effective as Spenser's archaic diction. But Wesley thought he saw a way of unlocking the sanctuary of *Paradise Lost.* "This difficulty," he said, "almost insuperable as it appears, I have endeavoured to remove in the following Extract: First, by omitting those lines which I despaired of explaining to the unlearned; and, Secondly, by adding short and easy notes; such as, I trust, will make the main of this excellent poem clear and intelligible to any uneducated person of a tolerable good understanding."[12]

Milton must have stirred uneasily in his grave. Imagine the shade of the man who sought "fit audience though few,"—author of the poem which, above all other really great poems, calls upon all the wealth of bookish information the most scholarly reader can bring to it,—looking over Wesley's shoulder as he wrote his preface. The ghost of Milton was friendly towards Blake a few years later; but how he must have chattered with rage, in 1763, to see "short and easy notes; such as, I trust, will make the main of this excellent poem clear to any uneducated person of tolerable good understanding." Wesley would doubtless have countered with his oft-repeated retort: "I care not who speaks but what is spoken."

Many of the things Milton spoke had long since been absorbed into Wesley's normal vocabulary; and now, as he said, "To those passages which I apprehend to be peculiarly excellent, either with regard to sentiment or expression, I have prefixed a star; and these, I believe, it would be worth while to read over and over, or even to commit to memory."[13] Actually, he placed an asterisk at the end as well as at the beginning of the recommended passages. Had any reader followed Wesley's suggestion literally and undertaken to memorize these, he would have set himself no small task, for nearly one fifth of the whole was so distinguished.

Mere abbreviation was apparently no part of Wesley's purpose. Although practically every page suffered some excision, so that in the whole work almost two thousand lines were struck out, a reason other than a desire for shortness can be assigned in nearly all cases.[14]

The overwhelming majority of the passages discarded were so treated on account of the strange proper names therein mentioned. Of the passage:

> Next *Chemos,* th' obscene dread of *Moabs* Sons,
> From *Aroer* to *Nebo,* and the wild
> Of Southmost *Abarim;* in *Hesebon*
> And *Horonaim, Seons* Realm, beyond
> The flowry Dale of *Sibma* clad with Vines,
> And *Eleale* to th' *Asphaltick* Pool,[15]

Wesley printed only the first line.

Because of this principle, many a resounding simile was refused its place. But sometimes a simile offended in other ways. Occasionally the simplicity of the omitted figure suggests that Wesley was suspicious of the too frequent employment of the Virgilian device. But more often his objection was obviously based on an appreciation of the difficulty an unlearned man would have in following the sense. Such, no doubt, was the ground on which he crossed out the exquisite comparison of the devils swarming to conclave:

> As Bees
> In spring time, when the Sun with *Taurus* rides,
> Poure forth thir populous youth about the Hive
> In clusters; they among fresh dews and flowers
> Flie to and fro, or on the smoothed Plank,
> The suburb of thir Straw-built Cittadel,
> New rub'd with Baume, expatiate and confer
> Thir State affairs. So thick the aerie crowd
> Swarm'd and were straitn'd.[16]

Long practice in abridging had made Wesley adept in converting long, involved sentences into short ones. A single example will show something of his method: the words in square brackets were deleted, leaving two perfect pentameter lines where three had been:

. . . our better part remains
To work [in close design,] by [fraud or] guile
What force effected not: that he [no less]
At length [from us] may find, who overcomes
By force, hath overcome but half his foe.[17]

In this and a very few other cases the omissions seem so entirely unnecessary that I suspect Wesley found in his task often the same sort of fascination that other people have seen in anagrams and cross-word puzzles.

In accordance with the statement in the Preface, nearly all the deletions in Wesley's Extract were made for the ostensible purpose of leaving the poem more universally understandable; a very few, however, are better accounted for by supposing that Wesley distrusted their theological or religious implications. It is notorious that Milton quite failed to "justify the ways of God to men;" Wesley would not have said he completely failed, but he was aware that some men would see a contradiction in the nature of a God who left Satan to do what he would,

That with reiterated crimes he might
Heap on himself damnation, while he sought
Evil to others, and enrag'd might see
How all his malice serv'd but to bring forth
Infinite goodness, grace and mercy shewn
On Man by him seduc't, but on himself
Treble confusion, wrath and vengeance pour'd.[18]

He simply omitted the lines.

No matter what the reason for an omission was, Wesley took great care to preserve the general integrity of Milton's line. Usually when he began an excision within a verse, he closed it at a corresponding place in the measure of a subsequent verse. When that was not possible, he almost invariably caught step with the original by marking through the next non-essential word. So, when an omission left him with the potential Alexandrine:

Astarte, Queen of Heav'n. *Thammuz* came next behind,[19]

he dropped the last word. Only on extremely rare occasions did he have to add a word to correct a fault his abridging had made in a verse. An example occurs in the place where the five syllables of "After these appear'd"[20] had to be trimmed to three: Wesley wrote, "Next appear'd."

The Notes at the end of each book were of various kinds. Most were short glossarial definitions of unusual or archaic words,[21] or identifications of names of men or places retained in the text.[22] Less frequently they contained supplementary information calculated to enliven the narrative. For example, there was an exceptionally long note appended to the statement: *"Thammuz came next*—Thammuz, or Adonis, was the god of the Sidonians, slain by a wild boar in Mount Lebanon, from which the river Adonis descends. At a certain season of the year, about the Feast of Adonis, this is of a bloody colour, occasioned by a sort of Minium or red earth, which the rains wash into it. The women then made loud lamentations for Adonis, supposing that it was discoloured with his blood." Once in a while Wesley put his own views into a comment: *"Can make a Heaven of Hell*—This is fit rant for a Stoic or a Devil."

If the *Extract from Milton's Paradise Lost* were the only extant record of the poem, its high rank among the epics of world literature would remain unchanged. He who knows the original would regret the loss of what Wesley cut away and find the excision of a few passages, such as the simile of the bees, utterly indefensible. But for the unlearned people whom the editor expected to reach, the edition was epochal. It brought them one of the greatest of all poems in a form which, though cleared of the thorns which would inevitably have discouraged them, showed them no scars where the pruning knife had cut. No part of the action was lost, and extremely few of the great memorable passages.

In 1770, sixteen years after he had infringed Robert Dodsley's copyright, Wesley published *An Extract from Dr. Young's Night Thoughts on Life, Death, and Immortality.* In so doing he laid himself open to a technical charge of untruthfulness, for he had promised Dodsley "not to print the same in any form whatever." The only defense possible would have been to assert that the intention of his promise was to assure the publisher he would not again trespass on his legal rights, and that since the copyright had expired now, the poem was public property, and might be exploited by anyone. However, it may be noted that the French biographer of Edward Young, W. Thomas,[23] says that Wesley's Extract was published "probablement avec une autorisation speciale." At any rate, there is no record that the publication brought on any trouble.

Something of Wesley's opinion of Young's poem may be seen in the quotation with which he opened his address to the reader: "It is the observation of a late ingenious writer that 'What is usually called a correct taste is very much offended with Dr. Young's "Night Thoughts". It is obvious that the poetry sometimes sinks into childish conceits, or prosaic flatness; but oftener rises into the turgid, or false sublime; and that it is often perplexed and obscure. Yet this work contains many strokes of nature and passion, which touch the heart in the most tender and affecting manner. Besides, there are afflictions too deep to bear either reasoning or amusement. They may be soothed, but cannot be diverted. The gloom of the "Night Thoughts" perfectly corresponds with this state of mind. It indulges and flatters the present passion, and at the same time presents those motives of consolation which alone can render certain griefs supportable. We may here observe that secret and wonderful endearment which nature has annext to all our sympathetic feelings, whereby we enter into the deepest scenes of distress and sorrow, with a melting softness of heart, far more delightful than all the joys which dissipating and unthinking mirth can inspire.' "[24]

Wesley found in the original poem much to regret and much to commend. The commendable qualities were sufficient to warrant his labor, and the regrettable to justify it. *Night Thoughts* not only shared with *Paradise Lost* frequent difficulties of comprehension; it suffered from glaring inequalities, of both subject-matter and execution. Although it is probably true that a well-integrated work of art suffers real injury if any of its component parts are knocked away, it is certainly true that the disgust roused by one false note in a poem impairs the reader's enjoyment of whatever beauty there may be in the surrounding lines. The *Night Thoughts* is not the sort of poem that suffers most seriously from the application of the pruning knife: the very title indicates its discursive nature, and invites one (if at all) rather to dip into its pages than to read straight through. No one is likely to disagree, in general, with Wesley's belief that much of the poem would better have been left unwritten.

It was in December of 1768 that Wesley set about preparing his version. "In the latter end of the month," he records, "I took some pains in reading over Dr. Young's *Night Thoughts,* leaving out the indifferent lines, correcting many of the rest, and explaining the hard words, in order to make that noble work more useful to all, and more intelligible to ordinary readers."[25]

As his preface stated, he held to a threefold design.

"(1.) To leave out all the lines which seem to me either to contain childish conceits, to sink into prosaic flatness, to rise into the turgid, the false sublime, or to be incurably obscure to common readers." In regard to difficult passages, Wesley followed precisely the procedure of his Milton abridgment. As always, he omitted statements with whose theology or moral sentiment he strongly disagreed. And the third *Night* he omitted entirely. An adequate summary, with documentary demonstration, of the grounds upon which he cut away passages as poor poetry would be too long to fit the nature of the present study: frequently the fault is bound up with a consideration of the context. It may be said, however, that the passages omitted from Wesley's extract are easily among the worst in the poem. In the actual process of abridging, be it observed, Wesley did not attempt by wholesale excision to rework the admirable passages of the *Night Thoughts* into a drastically short piece which should have little resemblance to the original. In adhering usually to the main outline, he was compelled to retain material liable to the objections he mentioned; but he endeavored to do so no more "than was necessary to preserve some tolerable connection between the preceding and following lines."[26]

"(2.) To explain the words which are obscure, not in themselves, but only to unlearned readers." The explanatory notes were austerely brief. A display of non-essential erudition was the last thing in the world Wesley would have found tempting. "It was no part of my design," he protested, "to explain any thing at large; but barely to put, as often as I could, a plain word for a hard one: and where one did not occur, to use two or three or as few as possible."[27] In cases which would have demanded a paragraph from a scholar, he used a phrase, depending for justification on a notice in his preface: "where the word added does not express the common meaning of the word, it often expresses the Doctor's peculiar meaning; who frequently takes words in a very uncommon, not to say improper sense."[28] Only seldom did Wesley go beyond the limit of two or three words. One of the longest glossarial notes told the reader that "The *Syrens* used to sing men to sleep, and then devour them."[29] Rarely Wesley interpreted a line. Young wrote:

> Then, and then only Adam's offspring quits
> The sage, and hero, of the fields and woods,
> Asserts his rank, and rises into man.

Wesley glossed the clause thus: "Then only man is wiser and braver than the fox and the lion."[30]

"(3.) To point out, especially to these [unlearned readers], by a single or double mark, what appear to me to be the sublimest strokes of poetry, and the most pathetic strokes of nature and passion." To designate the passages he wished especially to recommend, he put one or two asterisks at the beginning and a single square bracket (]) at the end.

Wesley knew that such a task as he proposed for himself was a difficult one, and he realized how far short of his own ideal the hurry consequent from his numerous other duties kept him. Yet, recognizing in the poem an element valuable and rare—akin to, if not a part of, that consolation which it is one of the functions of religion to impart to sorrowing people—he felt that the main thing was to get the *Night Thoughts,* in an intelligible form, into the hands of unlearned readers. Having done that, he was glad enough to wish for a better edition than his: "Let one that has more leisure and more abilities supply what is here wanting."[31]

A singular illustration of John Wesley's independent and excellent poetic taste is observable in his dealings with the work of George Herbert. In 1709, when Wesley was six years old, the thirteenth edition of *The Temple* appeared; and the fourteenth was not forthcoming until after his death, that is, in 1799.[32] But in 1773 Wesley published, on thirty-two duodecimo pages, *Select*

Parts of Mr. Herbert's Sacred Poems, a pamphlet containing twenty-three poems from *The Temple.*

Wesley's fondness for Herbert had manifested itself not only in the adaptations made for his hymn-books, but also in frequent quotation.[33] When he came to choose poems for his edition, he obviously picked his own personal favorites. "On what principle the selection was made," says Green, the bibliographer,[34] "does not readily appear." Indeed, one searches in vain for any argumentative or sermonizing purpose distinguishable from the purposes which actuated Herbert; but even though Wesley may not have been conscious of a definite principle (a possibility difficult to believe) his good taste guided him well.

Some of the poems, "Virtue" for example, were among those he had reconstructed for the hymn-book. They now appeared in their original phrasing. He made no alterations; he restricted even his passion for abridging to the deleting of certain stanzas from five of the poems—usually because they were either repetitious of an idea already expressed or marred by an unusual degree of obscurity. Some few deletions may be accounted for by supposing that Wesley disagreed with the sentiments involved. For instance, when, in "The Church-Porch", Herbert spends two stanzas expanding the adjuration "Play not for gain, but sport;" Wesley cuts them out, possibly because he looked with disfavor on all games of chance. Some other deleted stanzas he probably thought "trifling".

The book had neither preface nor notes; but as a judiciously chosen anthology it served then, as indeed it might serve now, as a pleasant introduction to one of the most enduring and intellectually appealing of English devotional poets.

The obvious solution to a simple little bibliographical problem in connection with this book points to a mildly interesting unrecorded event in Wesley's life. There are three gatherings, of six leaves each, signed, respectively, *B, C,* and *D.* Subtracting one leaf each for title-page and back fly-leaf, there are left sixteen leaves, or thirty-two pages, for text. Now the first twenty poems in the collection are in order as they appear in complete texts of *The Temple,* but the last three poems are drawn irregularly from places earlier in the complete text than is the twentieth. Apparently this is what happened: Wesley expected that the first twenty poems would make up a neat pamphlet. But when they had been set in type, the printer informed him that there was a space of something over three pages which could be filled at a negligible additional expense. Thereupon Wesley looked back over his unabridged text and chose three more poems of such a length as to extend to the bottom of the thirty-second page.

CHAPTER NINE

FICTION AND BIOGRAPHY

WESLEY was himself fond of narratives, both fictional and true, and he sought to afford his people the same pleasure. In *The Arminian Magazine* stories frequently appeared; some were records of Christian lives, some were tales the editor himself at least credited, and some were frankly spun out of the imagination. Even in *The Christian Library* he included an abridged version of Bunyan's *Holy War;* and two of his separately published books can quite definitely be called novels.

I

In 1743 he was carrying the campaign of the religious revival on wings of a fresh and fervent enthusiasm. Accompanied by startling and often terrifying phenomena, his sermons were compelling great multitudes to gather about him in the open air. Poor people—colliers, artizans, workers in manufacturing establishments that were already flourishing—found an unearthly compulsion in his words. He promised them a happiness in which they somehow believed; he ordered them to tasks which they somehow performed. It was a time of persecution. Magistrates and clergymen despised the Methodists for the indecorus manifestations of their emotional upheaval; and mobs, sometimes in the spirit of rough fun and sometimes in blind anger, threatened and executed physical violence upon them. The Methodists were a happy people, but their happiness was seasoned with a tight-lipped determination. Many difficulties besetting their Christian path were very real, quite material. And the preaching of John Wesley made the spiritual world in which their greatest struggles were pitched seem no less real and hardly less palpable.

Observing their valor and recording it with laconic satisfaction in his *Journal Extracts,* Wesley let his mind run back to the England of sixty years before, where another preacher to the poor, likewise under persecution, had made a book depicting the eventful life of a Christian. In *Pilgrim's Progress* John Bunyan had furnished his simple congregations with a vivid materialized reflection of their own difficulties and dear desires and inspired them to fight doggedly ahead on the road to heaven. The same book might well perform a similar function for Wesley's no less simple Methodists and at the same time help to lead them toward more and more reading.

Wesley seldom lost time in rendering his ideas in appropriate action. He began preparing an edition suitable to his purpose; and in 1743 his small volume was published.

It was a drastic abridgment. The people whom Wesley wanted to reach were distressingly poor, and many of them were unaccustomed as yet to purchasing books of any sort. Since distribution was contingent upon cheapness, he fixed the price at a hitherto unheard-of figure, fourpence. To scale down printing costs to meet such a price, extreme brevity was necessary. Entirely omitting part two, the somewhat inferior account of Christiana's pilgrimage, Wesley reduced part one so that it could be printed on his forty-nine duodecimo pages. An appalling amount of material gave way to the necessity for conserving space.

The "Author's Apology for his Book" (a sort of poetical foreword) and passages throughout in which people burst into song or verse, though quaint and in some degree interesting, were really poor poetry. Bunyan's extensive system of marginalia, moreover, which served the double purpose of furnishing an argument or outline for the allegory and of indicating pertinent scriptural texts, was not an essential part of the narrative. When Wesley cut away these features, he inflicted no great damage.

But when he invaded Bunyan's flowing prose, he touched the very heart of what has made *Pilgrim's Progress* a classic. In dialogue, where Bunyan had indicated the speaker after the manner of dramatists, then frequently repeated his name in the body of the paragraph, Wesley relied wholly on the former device. Redundances of every kind quite disappeared, and with them disappeared the leisurely charm of Bunyan's style. In the first paragraph of the narrative an example may be seen. The bracketed words Wesley omitted:

> And as I slept I dreamed [a Dream. I dreamed]; and behold, I saw a man cloathed with Rags—.

In cases where simple pruning would not suffice for the compression of a paragraph, Wesley felt free to paraphrase. For example, the original reads:[1]

> What! more fools still? Be ruled by me, go back; who knows whither such a brain-sick fool will lead you? Go back, go back, and be wise.

In the abridgment this becomes:[2]

> What! more fools still? Come back, come back. Who knows whither a Madman may lead you?

The result of this kind of abridging was a radical change in tempo. Where Bunyan was vigorous and straightforward, his abbreviated sentences become almost staccato. The intrinsic excellence of the plotted story, the simplicity of the allegorical fancies, the sturdy homeliness of the imaginative atmosphere are all indelibly Bunyan's. The manner of delivery became more nearly Wesley's: swift, direct, curt.

Even some of the incidents almost or altogether disappeared. The combat between Apollyon and Christian, and the trial and condemnation of Faithful in the court of Vanity are hardly recognizable in the telegraphic brevity of Wesley's phrasing; and some passages which by no stretch of the imagination can be called superfluous are nowhere to be found. Such, for example, are the following: Evangelist's description of Mr. Worldly Wiseman; Christian's endeavor to wake Sloth, Simple, and Presumption; the perils of Pope, Pagan, and the Old Man in the Cave; the incidents connected with By-Ends, Save-All, Money-Love, and Hold-the-World; and the view of the Celestial City which Christian and Hopeful beheld through the telescope of the Shepherds on the Delectable Mountains.

If Wesley had done nothing more than condense by omission and paraphrase, he would have left *Pilgrim's Progress* far different from the original. But by deliberately altering material therein, and adding new sentences and paragraphs of his own, he made it a frame for his own teaching and somewhat different in kind from Bunyan's work. For instance, one teaching that eighteenth-century religious thinkers had commonly come to regard as verging dangerously upon "enthusiasm", a doctrine which, though a part of the stated articles of orthodox Anglican faith, they seldom expounded, was Personal Assurance. It was partly by laying extraordinary emphasis upon this point that Wesley had estranged himself from his fellow clergymen. Bunyan had put into Faithful's mouth a long discussion of one evidence whereby man may discover the presence and activity of the Grace of God in his heart.[3] Wesley retained the suggestion, epitomized it in a short sentence, and added five other evidences.[4] Again, when Bunyan intimated that Christian must necessarily pass through the Valley of the Shadow of Death,[5] Wesley retained the sense of the original, but qualified it in a footnote: "N. B. I cannot learn, either from Scripture or experience that every Christian passes through this."

To say that, as a work of art, Wesley's abridgment is vastly inferior to the original would be expressing the truth in its mildest possible form. And yet the accepted opinion—"It cannot be called one of Wesley's successful works, however good his aim may have been"[6]—is not altogether a fair one. The little paper-bound booklet was immediately popular, and continued in such favor among the poor people for whom it was intended, that at least seven editions were printed during Wesley's lifetime.[7] Insofar as it brought a readable version of one of the greatest of all prose allegories to a large number of humble people who resembled those for whom it was originally written, and inasmuch as it spread the fame of the work among a class of people who were not long afterwards to raise themselves and their children to a place in the literary reading public, the mangled story of Christian cannot appear, to the eye of a literary historian, by any means an entirely contemptible performance.

II

When Henry Brooke's five-volume novel, *The Fool of Quality,* was first published, 1766-70, the *Monthly Review* had the following comment: "A performance enriched by genius, enlivened by fancy, bewildered with enthusiasm, and overrun with the visionary jargon of fanaticism. We wish the author would give us an abridgment, cleared from the sanctimonious rubbish by which its beauties are so much obscured. In its present state, it will be a favourite only with Behmenites, Herrnhutters, Methodists, Hutchinsonians, and some of the Roman Catholics."[8] What must have been his disgust if the reviewer had known that the author would soon give the actual work of abridging into the hands of John Wesley!

Wesley came upon *The Fool of Quality* shortly after its completion, but the whimsical title so prejudiced him that he threw the book aside as worthless. Some time later, however, he looked at it again, glanced over the first page, and was so thoroughly fascinated that he read the whole work.

Indeed, as he said, he was "a little disgusted with the spinning out of the story, so as to fill five volumes; and wished some of the digressions had been pared off, that it might have come within a reasonable compass."[9] But this disappointment (together, it is barely possible, with the *Monthly Review's* comment) was the germ of an idea. In a letter to the nephew and namesake of the author,[10] he said: "When I read over in Ireland *The Fool of Quality,* I could not but observe the design of it, to promote the religion of the heart, and that it was well calculated to answer that design. . . . Yet there seemed to me to be a few passages . . . which might be altered to the better; I do not mean so much with regard to the sentiments, which are generally very just, as with regard to the structure of the story, which seemed here and there to be not quite clear. I had at first thought of writing to Mr. Brooke himself, but I did not know whether I might take the liberty. Few authors will thank you for imagining you are able to correct their works. But if he could bear it and thinks it would be of any use, I would give another reading . . . and send him my thoughts without reserve just as they occur."[11]

The suggestion apparently found a hearty welcome, though it was received not exactly as Wesley had expected: "My uncle is deeply sensible of your very kind offer," so ran the reply, "and most cordially embraces it. He desires me to express the warmth of his gratitude in the strongest terms, and says he most cheerfully yields the volumes you mention to your superior judgment, to prune, erase, and alter as you please. He only wishes they could have had your eye before they appeared in public. But it is not yet too late. A second edition will appear with great advantage when they have undergone so kind a revisal. But he is apprehensive your time is so precious, that it may be too great an intrusion upon it, unless made a work of leisure and opportunity. Yet as you have proffered it, he will not give up the privilege, but hope leisure may be found for so friendly and generous a work."[12]

Given an entirely free hand, Wesley devoted to the abridgment some of the spare hours he found during the next few years, and in 1781 he published the result under a title which had been Brooke's subtitle: *The History of Henry, Earl of Moreland.* Henry Brooke's name was mentioned neither on the title-page nor in the preface. In the absence of any recorded explanation of the omission, we may resort to a conjecture that since Brooke was not at the time of publication in fit condition either to approve or to disapprove what had been done to his book, and since it was more radically altered than Wesley had first proposed, those who were concerned in the enterprise decided on silence as the kindest course to follow.

The audience for which Wesley designed this work was quite different from that to which he addressed his version of *Pilgrim's Progress.* During the decades intervening since that abridgment, the social and economic level of the Methodists had risen sharply. Sobriety, industry, and thrift had enabled members of the societies to occupy positions in the van of the movement which, through the operations of the industrial revolution, had opened a way for many of the more enterprising poor to achieve a respectable measure of affluence. The average prosperity of Methodist families was further elevated by the recruiting into the movement of many middle-class men and women. Though *Methodist* was still a term of contempt to most members of the wealthy and intellectual classes, it could no longer by any reach of fancy be used synonymously with hoodlum and pauper. Wesley was still, of course, interested in reclaiming the poor, degraded, and illiterate. But even as he had from the first attempted to provide artistic reading matter for those Methodists who could absorb it, he increased his efforts in this direction now that the number of his fully literate adherents had grown into the thousands.

As his audience for *Henry, Earl of Moreland* was different from that which bought *Pilgrim's Progress* for fourpence, so his manner of abridging changed. Formerly he had butchered a graceful creature of the imagination to serve up spiritual pabulum to coarse, uncultivated palates. Now he endeavored to relieve a work of art of the misshapen excrescences which disfigured it: his primary aim was to make *Henry, Earl of Moreland* simply a finer novel than *The Fool of Quality.*

He believed he had succeeded. After completing it, he praised his abridgment in terms which, incidentally, indicate his ideal for this sort of "treatise":

"I now venture to recommend the following treatise, as the most excellent of its kind of any that I have seen, either in English or in any other language. The lowest excellence therein is the style, which is not only pure in the highest degree; not only clear and proper, every word being used in its true, genuine meaning; but frequently beautiful and elegant, and, where there is room for it, truly sublime. But what is of far greater value, is, the admirable sense which is conveyed therein; as it sets forth, in full view, most of the important truths which are revealed in the Oracles of God. And these are not only well illustrated, but also proved in an easy, natural manner: so that the thinking reader is taught, without any trouble, the most essential doctrines of religion.

"But the greatest excellence of all in this treatise, is, that it continually strikes at the heart. It perpetually aims at inspiring and increasing every right affection; at the instilling gratitude to God, and benevolence to man. And it does this not by dry, dull, tedious precepts, but by the liveliest examples that can be conceived; by setting before your eyes one of the most beautiful pictures that was ever drawn in the world. The strokes of this are so delicately fine, the touches so easy, natural, and affecting, that I know not who can survey it with tearless eyes, unless he has a heart of stone. I recommend it, therefore, to all who are already, or desire to be, lovers of God and man."[13]

Wesley himself stated, in part, the extent of the pruning whereby he had brought the book to such commendable excellence: "This is now done, by retrenching at least one-third of what was published in those five volumes, more to the satisfaction of the bookseller than of the judicious reader.[14] I have omitted, not only all the uninteresting dialogues between the Author and his Friend, but most of the trifling and ludicrous incidents; which would give little entertainment to men of understanding. I likewise omit the remarks upon the feudal government, which are of little use to the generality of readers; as also great part of the Mystic Divinity, as it is more philosophical than scriptural."[15]

The "dialogues between the Author and his Friend," which are interspersed here and there throughout the course of the original narrative (usually at the heads of chapters), and the "remarks upon the feudal government," wherewith the author turned his novel for many solid pages into a dreary political essay, were but two instances of Wesley's customary action. Brooke had written a long Dedication to the Public, containing a series of moral dissertations on customs and manners; and a Preface which, departing from an explanation of why the hero is called a fool, discusses the varying significance of the word "folly". Wesley omitted both. Throughout the five volumes Brooke frequently inserted long philosophical disquisitions, sometimes strained into dialogue and sometimes frankly couched in essay form. A few of these Wesley retained, but most either went into the discard or suffered such abridgment and compression as would enable the reader to sustain through them the memory that he was reading a story.[16]

It was frankly upon religious grounds that Wesley omitted "great part of the Mystic Divinity." Mysticism, he believed, led to quietism; and quietism his energetic spirit abhorred. But there were other excisions also obviously made because of religious attitudes. For instance, if there was one point upon which Wesley was superlatively meticulous, it was his jealous care that the name and dignity of God should be held in inviolable reverence. Where the hero as a little child, according to Brooke, "beheld his patron [*i. e.* foster-father] as his father and his God,"[17] Wesley crossed out the last three words. He retained a retelling of the pagan story of Damon and Pythias, but deleted a clause therein which contained a wish for the gods to be propitious;[18] he apparently felt that the attribution of providential care to any power other than Jehovah was too close an approximation to sacrilege. Another interesting deletion was the statement in one place: "God had foreordained the means."[19]

Wesley claimed to have omitted "most of the trifling and ludicrous incidents, which would give little entertainment to men of understanding." On rare occasions these were a part of the main narrative thread; such was the case when Wesley skipped over a description of the sad plight of a cruel schoolmaster after the hero had successfully engineered an expedition of revenge against him: he was severely beaten and put naked in the street with his hands tied.[20] Far more frequently the "trifling incidents" were those auxiliary stories with which Brooke, in company with most of his contemporary novelists, obliterated the thread of his central plot.[21] Wesley did not by any means entirely eliminate even these. The several long narratives, those long enough to fill each a small volume by itself, he retained; but in such cases he wrought such a degree of compression as to make them quite definitely subsidiary to the main story.

The sense of delicacy which made a part of Wesley's nature was very becoming to him as a gentleman, a scholar, and a clergyman; but it neither blinded him to ugliness in life about him nor caused him to falsify the mirroring of art by emasculating the literature he abridged. In his dealings with *The Fool of Quality* this fact found striking exemplification. When indelicate statements tended merely to provoke laughter, he cut them out. Two cases from the episode of the youthful hero's relations with Vindex, the schoolmaster, will serve as illustrations. In the following passages Wesley marked through the bracketed words: After the boy had received a sound thrashing, "He had full time and leisure to contrive [with one end], a just and worthy retribution [for the sufferings of the other]."[22] Later, Mr. Fenton, the hero's foster-father, lecturing Vindex on the faults of schoolmasters, said: "They generally lay hold on the human constitution, [as a pilot lays hold of the rudder of a ship, by the tail,] by the single motive, [I say,] of fear [alone]."[23]

On the other hand, by retaining without alteration such episodes as that of Lord Stivers' attempt first to seduce, then to commit rape upon, Arabella Clement, he incurred the censure of more tender minded critics. For instance, the Rev. William Holden Hutton[24] says of the abridgment: "It is crowded with murders and rapes, overloaded with incident and excitement. . . . After reading this, and what he says of it, one is tempted to wonder whether Wesley had any literary conscience or any literary taste." As a matter of fact, in places where the book offered a serious criticism of life by painting it in sometimes unflattering colors, Wesley unhesitatingly set the seal of his approval.

Two curious changes in terms of appellation seem to indicate a dislike of the petty ridiculous. As a child, the future Earl's favorite way of addressing or speaking of his foster father was by use of the word "Dada". Almost but not quite always Wesley altered this to "Sir" when Harry was addressing him directly, and to "my father" when he spoke of him to other people. He also altered the name of Mr. Clement's son. In the original he is "Richard", and is usually called by the familiar contraction "Dicky"; Wesley's names for him are "Thomas" and "Tommy". The explanation must be that Wesley was aware of the various absurd word-plays that could be made on "Dicky" and was unwilling to evoke them. The New English Dictionary gives, among others, these two eighteenth-century meanings: "a he-ass" and "an under petticoat."

The cult of sensibility found ample expression in *The Fool of Quality*. Although Wesley did not alter the original atmosphere of highly charged emotionalism, he mercifully eliminated a large fraction of the faintings, hysterias, sighs, tears, kisses, and caresses. Even in his abridgment there are too many of these for twentieth-century taste, but in his hands the characters acquired a degree of moderation and restraint quite Spartan in comparison with their former demonstrativeness. Wesley knew from long experience that he who would call forth tears from hearers or readers does not himself necessarily have to weep.

Wesley acted upon the assumption that a book which is designed to give pleasure as well as instruction to the general reader should be intelligible within itself. He omitted Latin mottoes and phrases, learned or technical terms such as would be so much Greek to the average novel-reader, and allusions to other works and to the classical mythology with which he was himself so familiar.

By means of most of the devices we have been observing, Wesley sought to make his version of the novel more decorous, more wholesomely virile in its emotional tone, and more readily intelligible to people of ordinary culture and learning. But it was upon the structure that he expended his greatest care, and it was upon his treatment of that basic feature that he depended most largely for sculpturing an intrinsically better artistic unit out of the original work. To that end he sacrificed not only the small amount of material he found unworthy in itself, but also much philosophy that was agreeable with his own teachings, and many trains of incident which were, taken by themselves, equally good as some he preserved.

In point of structure Wesley's novel is more purely narrative than the original. In the words of an adverse critic, he was "impatient of reflection and extracted a moral meaning from the incident."[25] As a matter of fact, he conceived that there is a difference between the direct teaching of the sermon and the artistic didacticism of fiction. He not only pared away a great deal of the encumbering, soporific moralizing and philosophic speculation, but by compressing the incidental stories he emphasized the main plot and made its outline clearer.

The fifth volume of the original novel provides a striking illustration of Wesley's partiality for the central story. The first hundred pages contained only one interruption[26] in the course of a uniquely long passage of straight narration. With the exception of that one interruption, which altogether disappeared, Wesley here exercised his abridging pen hardly at all. Not only did he depart from his usual custom by retaining every paragraph; but this is the only section of the whole work where he did not strike out a word or a phrase or two in nearly every sentence. After the hundredth page, moral sayings began to occur again in long paragraphs; and Wesley returned to his usual, trenchant method.

Wesley did not convert Brooke's episodic plot structure into that unified design which is sometimes called dramatic structure. He did not even leave it tightly bound and consecutively motivated. But he did reduce the rambling mass of disconnected, incoherent, and heterogeneous matter into a semblance of order. He whose pleasure in novels is based upon an interest rather in story than in the history of bypaths of philosophic thought, therefore, will prefer *Henry, Earl of Moreland* to *The Fool of Quality*.

Wesley's abridgment went through at least seven editions.[27] But though it was for a long time popular, it brought upon its editor much adverse criticism. As Tyerman, half agreeing, says, "That an old evangelist, like Wesley bordering on forescore years of age, should revise, abridge, publish, and circulate a novel, has always been a perplexity to a certain section of Wesley's admirers."[28]

Indeed, Wesley was careful to avoid making an unreserved recommendation of novel-reading. It was a habit, he thought, whose acquisition might prove harmful to children. "I should recommend very few novels to young persons, for fear they should be too desirous of more"; so, quaintly and half humorously, ran his answer to a school-teacher's inquiry if there were "any unexceptionable novels besides *The Fool of Quality.*" "Mr. Brooke wrote one more (besides the *Earl of Moreland*), *The History of the Human Heart.* I think it well worth reading; though it is not equal to his former production. The want of novels may be supplied by well-chosen histories."[29]

And yet he felt nothing but pity for those who could not enjoy a feeling of sympathy with fictional characters. One John Easton, a Methodist itinerant preacher, took it upon himself to condemn Wesley for publishing *Henry, Earl of Moreland.* Wesley listened to him patiently, then quizzed him about two episodes in the book.

"Wesley.—'Did you read Vindex, John?'

"Easton.—'Yes, sir.'

"Wesley.—'Did you *laugh,* John?'

"Easton.—'No, sir.'

"Wesley.—'Did you read Damon and Pythias, John?'

"Easton.—'Yes, sir.'

"Wesley.—'Did you *cry,* John?'

"Easton.—'No, sir.'

"Wesley, lifting up his eyes, and clasping his hands, exclaimed: 'O earth—earth—earth!' "[30]

A common notion of Wesley's nature is one expressed by Leslie Stephen:[31] "His emotions impel him to vigorous action; and are much too serious to be cultivated for their own sakes or to be treated aesthetically." Wesley's emotions did impel him to vigorous action, and they were serious to the point of being inextricably bound up with the most important of all considerations.

But, far from repressing or ignoring the aesthetic cultivation of emotion, he delighted in the literature which best served that end; and he strove to overcome that misplaced asceticism which, as it tended to close the minds of his people against the great world of ideas, hardened their hearts against the impulses of beauty.

III

It would be a mistake for one moment to forget that every activity in which Wesley engaged had its source in the ruling passion of his life and was therefore directed toward extending the kingdom of God in the hearts of men. Even the novels were edited and published to attract sinning people to the Christian life. If fictional characters and events of the fancy were able to woo men to Godliness, how much more direct and lively exhortations could be found in the true narratives of good men's lives!

Long before he devoted large sections of the *Arminian Magazine* to Lives and Letters, he published similar and sometimes more extended accounts in single volumes. The Lives were originally written by friends of the persons so distinguished. But Wesley also edited and published a variety of journals and letters wherein the writers spoke for themselves. He believed that rendering personal testimony of the goodness and power of God ought to be considered a duty by Christian people. "In writing the lives and characters of eminent men," he said in his *Life of Fletcher,* "the Roman Catholics have a great advantage over us. The pious members of the Church of Rome make a conscience of concealing any thing from their directors, but disclose to them all the circumstances of their lives, and all the secrets of their hearts: whereas very few of the Protestants disclose to others, even their most intimate friends, what passes between God and their own souls; at least not of set purpose. Herein they forget, or at least disregard, that wise remark of the ancient writers: (exactly agreeable to various passages that occur in the canonical Scriptures:) "It is good to conceal the secrets of a king, but to declare the loving-kindness of the Lord.' "[32]

It must not be thought that Wesley approved of the Roman confessional. What he desired was the narration of such spiritual incidents as might be made public for the encouragement and edification of all men.

Some of the pious works Wesley published had been in print before. But most of them, called forth by the revival he led, would never have gone abroad except for him. The rhetorical and grammatical condition in which they reached Wesley's hands is unknown. He saw something worthy in them, however, worked over them, corrected their solecisms, wrought them into a semblance of form, and sent them out to inspire other men and women to love a holy life and die a joyous, triumphant death.[33]

Wesley himself prepared the most graceful of the pious Lives. John Fletcher, vicar of Madeley, was one of the best-loved men who figured prominently in the great revival. A native of Switzerland, he had been educated on the continent, had come under Methodist influence in England, and had shortly thereafter taken holy orders in the Established Church. Drawn into the bitter disputes of the times, he proved himself the gentlest of controversial writers; Wesley himself, in speaking of an argumentative piece of his own, said: "I wish I may have done it with the inimitable sweetness and gentleness that Mr. Fletcher has done. His letters (vilely as they have been misrepresented) breathe the very spirit of the gospel. You might read them to learn how to return good for evil, to bless them that curse you."[34] The incident in Fletcher's life which has always seemed most characteristic of him occurred during a sermon. A robin flew near him and perched, distracting the attention of his hearers and utterly ruining the effect of his pre-prepared discourse. He immediately dropped the thread of his original idea, took the robin as a text, and preached a memorable sermon on the love of God.

This was the man to whose keeping Wesley desired eventually to give over the leadership of Methodism. But Fletcher died first, in 1785, and it devolved upon Wesley to preach his funeral sermon. Resolved to write a biography, he began supplementing what he had said in this discourse. He procured what material he could from people who had known Fletcher intimately at various stages of his career,[35] and then shut himself up some months to give undivided attention to his task.[36] In December, 1786, he published *A Short Account of the Life and Death of the Rev. John Fletcher.*

The form of this work was peculiar. In the preface Wesley told his readers: "You may easily observe, that . . . I am little more than a compiler; for I owe a great, if not the greatest part of the ensuing tract to a few friends, who have been at no small pains in furnishing me with materials; and above all my dear friend, (such she has been almost from her girlhood,) Mrs. Fletcher. I could easily have altered both hers and their language, while I retained their sentiments; but I was conscious I could not alter it for the better; and I would not alter it for altering' sake; but judged it fairest to give you most of their accounts, very nearly in their own words." He adhered to the promise of his announcement and narrated the story of Fletcher's life as if, having gathered and sorted a number of fragmentary accounts, he were reading them to a group of friends, and linking them together in the informal style of an ordinary conversation.

Some of the material he supplied from his own experience; for, as he said, "No man in England has had so long an acquaintance as myself. Our acquaintance began almost as soon as his arrival in London, about the year 1752, before he entered into holy orders, or, I believe, had any such intention; and it continued uninterrupted between thirty and forty years, even till it pleased God to take him to himself. Nor was ours a slight or ordinary acquaintance; but we were of one heart and of one soul. We had no secrets between us for many years; we did not purposely hide any thing from each other."[37] In spite of his modest statement, it is true that the incidents and traits Wesley described from his own recollections are the most charming parts of the book.

Wesley was aware that among many people of education and sophistication, certain elements in the religious beliefs he held were thought quaint, archaic, vestigial remnants of an age when ignorance had not yet been beaten back by the clear light of reason; but he cheerfully clung to his convictions. Occurrences which admitted of a perfectly natural explanation he persisted in viewing as the special interposition of providential power. Whenever a good man had a narrow escape from misfortune, he saw in the "remarkable deliverance" evidence of the hand of God setting aside normal, natural laws. If the eighteenth century found such opinions inconsistent with their modern common-sense rationalism, how much more strangely do they strike the ear of the twentieth century! One is tempted to think sometimes that Wesley was engaging in a bit of very dry humor; but doubtless he wrote out such incidents as the following in all seriousness:

Fletcher and his companions had just arrived in England and passed through the customs. "From hence they went to an inn; but here they were under another difficulty. As they spoke no English they could not tell how to exchange their foreign into English money; till Mr. Fletcher going to the door, heard a well dressed Jew talking French. He told him the difficulty they were under, with regard to the exchange of money. The Jew replied, 'Give me your money, and I will get it changed in five minutes.' Mr. Fletcher without delay gave him his purse, in which were ninety pounds. As soon as he came back to his company he told them what he had done. They all cried out with one voice, "Then your money is gone. You may never expect to see a crown or a doit of it any more. Men are constantly waiting about the doors of these inns, on purpose to take in young strangers." Seeing no remedy, no way to help himself, he could only commend his cause to God. And that was enough;—before they had done breakfast, in came the Jew, and brought him the whole money."[38]

Partially because of such old-fashioned passages as these, the *Life of Fletcher* has long since lost its public; but when Wesley speaks of a trait such as is still valued by humanity, the graciousness of his words still carries the appeal they had at first: "I think one talent wherewith God had endued Mr. Fletcher has not been sufficiently noted yet: I mean his courtesy; in which there was not the least touch either of art or affectation. It was pure and genuine, and sweetly constrained him to behave to every one (although particularly to inferiors) in a manner not to be described, with so inexpressible a mixture of humility, love, and respect. . . . Never did any man more perfectly suit his whole behaviour to the persons and the occasion."[39]

Good biographies, of course, have an aesthetic appeal at least as universal as good novels. But Wesley's *Life of Fletcher* and the various Lives, Letters, and Journals he edited served a purpose too exclusively applicable to contemporary circumstances to endure. They have some historic interest; they form an important part of a great educative and emotional movement. But so far as the present reader of general literature is concerned, they may well be permitted to join most of the medieval Saints' Lives in a long, long rest, unopened and unknown.

CHAPTER TEN

POLITICAL WRITINGS

JOHN WESLEY made no original contribution to political theory. He did not even embrace a political philosophy which was logically sound or self-consistent. Except when the king was under attack, he generally avoided bringing political considerations into his sermons, and he directed his preachers similarly to abstain.[1] He seemed almost unaware of the power of government to bring about social reform; for in all his efforts to alleviate the conditions of the underprivileged, like Jane Addams in our own day, he never actively solicited the aid of Parliament and rarely urged the necessity for legal action in remoulding the world of the common man. That is strange; for it was in great part the spirit he woke in England that motivated the reforms of the next century, and it was by means of the system of organization whose power he revealed to them that the lower classes made their voice effective in Parliament.[2]

Wesley was more vitally concerned with direct reform of the individual. Even in his pamphlet *Free Thoughts on the Present State of Public Affairs* (1770), whose title would lead one to expect a constructive critical estimate of governmental policies, his emphasis rests upon questions of private and social rather than public and political morality. He disclaims any ability to offer a panecea for the ills of the nation, and ridicules the Englishman's habit of believing that, however obscure his station in life, he can pass judgment upon the great affairs of state. Wesley himself shows a clear apprehension of the questions before Parliament; but contents himself, after defending the king from certain imputations of misconduct, with pointing out causes of unrest which are only secondarily manifest in political measures: greed, luxury, pride, and other moral faults which, to the degree that they possess a people, will find reflection, on a greater scale, in its government.

On at least one occasion, however, he entered a not very hopeful plea for laws which should effect relief of widespread distress. In the early months of the year 1773, after observing an unusually great scarcity of food and a corresponding increase in dire hunger among the poor, he wrote and published *Thoughts on the Present Scarcity of Provisions.* After reviewing the causes of high prices, he proposed a series of practical measures by which a juster balance could be established between the income of the lower classes and the cost of necessities. Among these were: provision for creating jobs; prohibition of the use of food grains in distilling liquors; taxation of certain luxuries; and reduction of general taxation by the discharge, in part, of the National Debt. But in his final sentences, hopeless of actually having such measures soon adopted, he indicates the point of attack upon which he threw the whole force of his life: "But will this ever be done? I fear not; at least we have no reason to hope for it shortly; for what good can we expect . . . for such a nation as this, where there is no fear of God; where there is such a deep, avowed, thorough contempt of all religion as I never saw, never heard or read of, in any other nation, whether Christian, Mahometan, or Pagan."[3]

Though Wesley despaired of writing social reformation into the statute books of England until the spirit of her people had been recreated more nearly in the image of his Master, he did not fail to interpret that desirable spirit in terms of conduct and in respect to existing problems.

In 1772 he read a book "by an honest Quaker," undoubtedly Anthony Benezet, "on that execrable sum of all villainies, commonly called the Slave-trade. I read of nothing like it in the heathen world, whether ancient or modern; and it infinitely exceeds, in every instance of barbarity, whatever Christian slaves suffer in Mahometan countries."[4] Impressed by the moral degradation inherent in the traffic, he at once allied himself with the very few other men of prominence who were bold enough and humane enough to denounce so lucrative an industry: in 1774 he published his famous and powerful tract, *Thoughts upon Slavery.*

This little book partook largely of the spirit of Rousseau, though Wesley would have hotly denied direct or indirect indebtedness. The idyllic picture of man in a state of nature, unspoiled by the vices of civilization, and living peaceably in his orderly villages, he paints in glowing colors. Horribly contrasted with this pleasant scene is a vivid description of every conceivable kind of brutality herewith white men could have debased themselves and tortured the negro. Since Wesley had very little first-hand knowledge of what he was writing about, he shows a tendency to state as fact much that proceeded from his own or someone else's lurid fancy. But since other Englishmen knew as little of the real state of affairs as he did, the pamphlet was well received and praised for its accuracy.[5]

The purpose of *Thoughts upon Slavery* was not to stimulate legislation. Wesley made his appeal, purely on moral and religious grounds, to those who were in any way connected with the trade; he exhorted them in the name of God to risk financial ruin rather than pursue further an occupation which would be the ruin of their souls and which would bring down upon them the avenging wrath of a God who cared for every man, however humble.

To be sure, Wesley powerfully and directly seconded the efforts of men like Wilberforce and Howard, who agitated for humanitarian reform through the use of political machinery—when Wilberforce was about to carry his anti-slavery program before Parliament, he received a virile, energetic letter of encouragement; it was the last letter the aged Wesley ever wrote. But so far as the work he himself initiated was concerned, Wesley concentrated his efforts upon something more fundamental than reform legislation and, in his opinion, anterior to it. He tried, with some success, so to condition the conscience of Englishmen that laws calculated to enforce the humane ethic of Jesus, as he understood it, would find the people ready and eager with their support.

After all, John Wesley was primarily a clergyman. The immediate province of his labor was in the souls of individual men; and to that province he devoted his best efforts.

Nevertheless, Wesley was a citizen of England, and as such he was profoundly concerned with political life. As a public character he made his influence felt, and as a writer he made his voice heard in the tumult of party bickerings, revolutionary demands, and reactionary broadsides. He was, by virtue of hereditary influence and the natural sympathies of his autocratic spirit, a staunch Tory; and the weight of his influence was thrown almost wholly on the side of conservatism—insofar as conservatism meant the maintenance and extension of British liberty under the law of the king.

In human affairs, to have a theory without carrying it into action was foreign to Wesley's nature. It was, therefore characteristic of him that his first political publication, *A Word to a Freeholder* (1747), should be a plea to voters, calling upon them to beware of bribery, and cast their ballot for that candidate who most clearly loved God, king, and country.

But even as the proper procedure from a good theory is action, the procedure likely to ensue from a bad theory is, likewise, action. Consequently, political ideas which tended toward the overthrow of existing institutions must be combatted argument for argument. Wesley feared the spread of democracy as he feared the plague. Twice in 1772 he brought out pamphlets. The first *Thoughts upon Liberty,* implying that those who followed Wilkes in crying for liberty were seeking to throw off all the restraints of law and decency, caught step with the reactionary trend and asserted that Englishmen ought, rather than raise a foolish cry for liberty, to give thanks for their privilege in possessing greater real liberty than any other people in the world. The second, *Thoughts Concerning the Origin of Power,* with the specious logic of a *reductio ad absurdum,* sought to demolish the growing furor of demands for recognition of the proposition that the source of governmental powers lies in the people governed.[6]

When Dr. Price, the famous Unitarian minister, issued *Observations on the Nature of Civil Liberty, the Principles of Government, and the Justice and Policy of the War with America,* Wesley was alarmed. Believing that Dr. Price's principles, "if practised, would overturn all government and bring in universal anarchy," he replied with *Some Observations on Liberty* (1776).[7] He was now, in part, on surer ground. Dr. Price had asserted that the population of the country had decreased and that the vitality of trade was at a low ebb. In the absence of a governmental census, John Wesley was, because of the evangelistic journeys he continually made to every part of the island, the one man in England best able to give judgment in matters like these; and his diligent inquiries had revealed that population was actually increasing and that trade was undergoing rapid expansion throughout the kingdom. Wesley, moreover, had informed himself carefully about the American situation, and was able to deliver a good account of himself as a defender of the government's policies. Even in combatting the democratic tenets of Dr. Price he took a position hard to refute: he appealed to history in supporting his contention that "there is most liberty of all, civil and religious, under a limited monarchy, there is usually less under an aristocracy, and least of all under a democracy."[8]

When agitation over the American situation was in its earlier stages, Wesley was in sympathy with the colonists and joined with those who sought to secure for them what they demanded. But when he was prevailed upon to believe that American demands and threats were but parts of a grand republican plot to overthrow the existing government of Great Britain, he made an about-face and set himself wholeheartedly with the Tory administration. In three energetic pamphlets[9] he urged uncompromising severity against those who had stirred up the trouble, and called on all men to join loyally with the government in its efforts to stamp out the menace at home and abroad. In 1776, when the unsuccessful campaigns in America were combining with other reverses to spread alarm among the people of Great Britain, and when many men were painting so gloomy a picture of national affairs as to imply that ruin and destruction were imminent, Wesley again went before the public. His two pamphlets, one addressed to Englishmen[10] and one to Irishmen,[11] were designed to show that England was still in a sound condition politically, and that her armies were quite able to cope with those of America and France.

In spite of his general confidence in the British armies, however, Wesley entered into those repeated and frequently justified attacks upon the conduct of the commanders who were carrying on the American War which were so blatant an indication of a blundering colonial policy. The lethargy of the British generals, whose indolence and inefficiency so often gave point to the demands of men who wished to let the colonies have their independence, angered him not a little. To this bitter controversy he contributed three publications, all extracted from earlier writers.[12] These, as well as Wesley's less personal original writings, were motivated by his desire at all costs to keep the colonies within the empire.

Most famous and important of all Wesley's political publications, the *Calm Address to our American Colonies,* is hardly less significant as a strange piece of literary work than it is as an historical document.

According to his own confession, Wesley was sympathetic with American political desires until he "read a tract, entitled 'Taxation no Tyranny'."[13] Indeed there is sufficient evidence of his earlier attitude in statements made publicly[14] and privately.[15] But Dr. Johnson's pamphlet did away with this Whiggish tendency and brought him back into the fold of severe Toryism. Then, he said, "As soon as I received more light myself, I judged it my duty to impart it to others."[16] Accordingly, he proceeded to extract the chief arguments from Johnson's treatise and recast them in a more popular form.

A hurried glance at the *Calm Address* would lead one to think it is largely the result of straight abridgment, wherein the editor merely deleted passages ranging in length from a word to several pages. Many passages are, in fact, copied out verbatim, but in most of the passages retained there are enough minor changes to show that Wesley departed from his usual method of pruning: it seems clear that he wrote out the *Calm Address* in full.

The most immediately obvious difference between *Taxation no Tyranny* and the *Calm Address* is in length. Condensation occurs throughout, but the greatest part of the eliminated material was in Johnson's opening sections. Wesley completely omitted several thousand words of philosophical political theory, and began abruptly: "Brethren and Countrymen,—1. The grand question which is now debated (and with warmth enough on both sides,) is this, Has the English parliament a right to tax the American colonies?" Brevity, however, was not his chief concern; he added at the end of a considerable section of his own with no source in Johnson.

Taxation no Tyranny was a general essay with a particular application. The *Calm Address* was, as indicated by the title, a direct appeal to the American people. Couched prevailingly in the second person, its arguments are balanced against hypothetical remarks supposed to proceed from an American patriot. "You say" so and so, was Wesley's way of setting up the target for a cannonade.

The direct manner of this almost conversational style of argument was an old device, but it fitted nicely the exigencies of the present situation. Wesley made the phrasing harmonize with his informal approach. Johnson's prose style in *Taxation no Tyranny* was not cumbersome, nor was it loaded down with a superfluity of learned words; but even so it admitted of considerable simplification. Wesley shortened sentences, replaced rounded periods with curt phrases,—in short, he made the pamphlet seasier to read and more rapid in tempo.

Wesley's concluding paragraphs, in addition to reinforcing Johnson's arguments by the citation of a series of laws and charters, contain a peculiar explanation of the causes leading to American unrest. Some Englishmen who hated monarchy had, he supposed, stirred up unsuspecting men in both England and America, with a view to effecting the separation of the colonies. The result of a successful secession would be to disgust all other Englishmen with the established government. Then, while troops were away in America, a successful revolution at home might be engineered.[17] Wesley brought his tract to a close with a warning to the Americans not to be duped by republican agitators, and with a characteristic appeal for them to join their English brothers in putting away their sins, fearing God, and honoring the king.[18]

The pamphlet roused a furor in circles where already excitement was at a high pitch.

It did not reach the people for whom it was expressly written. Wesley regretted that "The ports being just then shut up by the Americans I could not send it abroad as I designed."[19] The actual circumstances Wesley apparently did not know. They are described by Southey: "Such, indeed, was the temper of the Americans, that a friend to the Methodists got possession of all the copies of the *Calm Address* which were sent to New York, and destroyed them, foreseeing the imminent danger to which the preachers [*i. e.* the Methodist preachers and missionaries in America] would be exposed, if a pamphlet so unpopular in its doctrines should get abroad."[20] The *Calm Address,* therefore, had no opportunity for the direct exercise of its tranquillizing powers in America. But reports spread from England; and so well known did Wesley's conversion to the Tory side of the American question become, and so well recognized was the force of his influence with his own people, that the American Methodists were throughout the war regarded with suspicion; the preachers in particular were obnoxious to revolutionary patriots.[21]

It was in England that the *Calm Address* created a sensation. In three weeks the press had turned out forty thousand copies;[22] and "Within a few months fifty, or perhaps an hundred thousand copies, in newspapers and otherwise, were dispersed throughout Great Britain and Ireland;"[23] so Wesley admitted himself. "During several publishing seasons," records Trevelyan, "the great preacher was exposed to hailstorms of wild calumny, and unsavoury abuse. He was furiously denounced as a wolf in sheep's clothing; a Jesuit and a Jacobite unmasked; a chaplain in ordinary to the Furies; and a Minister Extraordinary to Bellona, the Goddess of War."[24] As the Whigs bastinadoed Wesley, the Tories praised and thanked him. "The government," it is elsewhere noted, "were so pleased with his little tract that copies were ordered to be distributed at the doors of all the metropolitan churches."[25]

There were four specific charges which stood out clearly amidst the general villification of his opponents: that he had plagiarized Dr. Johnson's pamphlet, that he looked for a pension or for preferment in the Church, that he was a turncoat, and that he sought to inflame men's minds.

Whether Wesley received Johnson's permission to publish his reworking of *Taxation no Tyranny* or not is unknown, but the incident caused no break in the friendliness existing between the two men. On the contrary, in a letter to Wesley dated February 6, 1776, Johnson wrote: "I have thanks likewise to return for the addition of your important suffrage to my argument on the American question. To have gained such a mind as yours may justly confirm me in my own opinion. What effect my paper has had upon the public I know not; but I have no reason to be discouraged. The lecturer was surely in the right, who, though he saw the audience slinking away, refused to quit the chair while Plato staid."[26] If Johnson's purpose was really to impress public opinion, rather than gain credit for doing so, he may well have been thankful for the *Calm Address*. He complained to Boswell that *Taxation no*

Tyranny neither sold well nor provoked the compliment of counter-attack; but everyone knew the powerful impact of the shorter argument: "Wesley's little tract probably reached a hundred readers where Johnson's labored and magisterial discussion reached one."[27]

Although Johnson's paper was published anonymously, Wesley's failure to mention his indebtedness in his first edition laid him open to fair attacks; they came promptly. In the preface to his next edition he disclaimed plagiarism by crediting *Taxation no Tyranny* with being the effective force which brought him to his present opinion and by acknowledging it as the source of his main arguments.[28]

The charge that he wrote the pamphlet for worldly gain was a serious one. Wesley did, indeed, receive a visit from a responsible official of the government, who asked him whether he would receive a reward, either in his own person or on behalf of his family. Declining, Wesley said that he "looked for no favours, and only desired the continuance of civil and religious privileges." By way of acknowledging the refusal, the emisary made another offer: "In all probability, sir," he said, "you have some charities which are dear to you; by accepting £ 50 from the privy purse, to appropriate as you may deem proper, you will give great pleasure to those for whom I act." That was too much for Wesley, who had an ever ready hand for gifts to be distributed among the poor. He accepted. Later, thinking of the church doors that were closed against him, he humorously told Dr. Adam Clarke he was "sorry that he had not requested to be made a royal missionary, and to have the privilege of preaching in every church."[29]

But such men as Horace Walpole asserted that "The artful patriarch of the Methodists . . . had produced the 'Calm Address' in order to court his patron, Lord Dartmouth; since he probably hoped either for a deanery or a bishopric."[30] Wesley took these and like accusations literally. He replied that his purpose was "Not to get money. Had that been my motive, I should have swelled it into a shilling pamphlet and have entered it at Stationers' Hall. Not to get preferment for myself or my brother's children. I am a little too old to gape after it for myself; and if my brother or I sought it for them, we have only to show them to the world. Not to please any man living, high or low. I know mankind too well. I know that they that love you for political service love you less than their dinner, and they that hate you hate you worse than the devil."[31]

The charge that he was a turncoat Wesley admitted, justifying himself on the ground that a man has the right to change his mind.

He vehemently denied any intention to stir up strife. "Least of all," said he, "did I write to inflame any: just the contrary. I contributed my mite toward putting out the flame that rages all over the land. This I have more opportunity of observing than any other man in England. I see with pain to what an height this already rises in every part of the nation. And I see many pouring oil into the flame by crying out, 'How unjustly, how cruelly the King is using the poor Americans, who are only contending for their liberty and for their legal privileges.'"[32] But he must have been distinctly blind if he had not seen that calmness was no part of the result ensuing from his *Address*.

What he really looked for was an ultimate effect. If all he hoped for had come to pass—if England had united solidly with George III, if America had been persuaded to submit to royal rule or had been subdued,—historians today would perhaps point Wesley out as one who was instrumental in checking a great and disastrous upheaval. In regard to the American question, he was dedicated to the *status quo;* and if that could be maintained, offending and enraging a few insurgents would be an unavoidable, insignificant necessity.

He was at least sincere. "England," he said when preparing additions to the *Calm Address,* "England is in a flame!—a flame of malice and rage against the King, and almost all that are in authority under him. I labour to put out this flame. Ought not every true patriot to do the same?"[33] His private expressions were exactly in accordance with his public protestations. In a private letter to his friend Thomas Rankin, dated London, October 20, 1775, he wrote as follows: "A paper was sent to me lately, occasioned by the troubles in America; but it would not do good. It is abundantly too tart; and nothing of that kind would be of service now. All parties are already too much sharpened against each other; we must pour water, not oil, into the flame. I had written a little tract upon the subject before I knew the American ports were shut up. I think there is not one sharp word therein; I did not design there should. However, many are excessively angry, and would burn me and it together."[34]

In reference to the American grievances and his wish that the colonies should remain a part of the empire, Wesley was for once at odds with the temper of his time, and here he was dealing with forces he could by no means direct. England remained prevailingly Whig, and America went her own way. Although it must be granted that the *Calm Address* was an effective piece of controversial writing, far more effective than Dr. Johnson's essay, the effectiveness was highly unfortunate. The only measurable results were an increase of party bitterness within England, a temporary augmentation of the anger which extended across the Atlantic, and a multiplication of Methodist difficulties in America. Moreover, if it is true, as Lecky declares, that the pamphlet had "a considerable influence in forming public opinion hostile to all concession,"[35] Wesley shares a grave responsibility. Without the support of a fairly large body of public opinion, the Tory government might have hesitated to persevere in an armed conflict. If that may be supposed, what Wesley actually "contributed his mite" towards was the total of effective causes which brought about and prolonged the American Revolutionary War.

The lasting importance of Wesley's beneficient influence upon political life lay rather in his power over the spirit of the English people, his stimulation of a conscience that became political, than in his direct pleas for specific governmental policies. Taken in the large, his political writings were among his least fortunate ventures.

CHAPTER ELEVEN

INSTRUCTIONAL WRITINGS

WESLEY considered himself a teacher of his people as well as a minister to their spiritual needs. In one sense, nearly all the volumes he distributed among Methodists served an educational purpose, for they stimulated an appreciation of the value of the written word in men and women who, left to the direction of their own naturally incurious dispositions, would seldom or never have turned a page. But Wesley prepared a number of books for purposes of giving definite and specific instruction in realms of learning which he considered important.

It was he who chose textbooks for the school which he and Whitefield established at Kingswood. For one reason or another he found it necessary often to replace or supplement the books available for teachers. In such cases he supplied the needs himself, either by judiciously editing texts already in existence or by writing new ones. He was interested in young children as well as the more mature: he prepared *Instructions for Children* and *Lessons for Children* as well as a necessarily abstruse *Compendium of Logick.*

Turning his expert knowledge in the field to good advantage, he was particularly concerned with supervising the study of languages. He wrote grammars of the English, French, Greek, Hebrew, and Latin tongues, and tried to keep them abreast of the latest developments.[1]

Wesley agreed most heartily with the opinion of the eighteenth century that an educated man should be intimately conversant with Latin. But, he said, "Elegance of style is not to be weighed against purity of heart; purity both from the lusts of the flesh, the lusts of the eye, and the pride of life. Therefore, whatever has any tendency to impair that purity is not to be tolerated, much less recommended, for the sake of that elegance. But of this sort (I speak not from the reason of the thing only, nor from my single experience) are the most of the classics usually read in great schools; many of them tending to inflame the lusts of the flesh (besides Ovid, Virgil's *Aeneid*, and Terence's *Eunuch*), and more to feed the lust of the eye and the pride of life."[2] Nothing of this kind would be incorporated in the Kingswood curriculum. He took as his motto a caution of Juvenal, whom, incidentally, he called "one of the most immodest wretches who ever defiled paper:"

> Nil dictu faedum, visuque haec limina tangat,
> Intra quae puer est.[3]

Though Wesley's first care was for the purity of the ideas contained in Latin authors, he was also jealous for the purity of literary style. He complained of the English schools: "There are exceedingly few wherein the scholars are thoroughly instructed even in the Latin and Greek tongues. They are not likely to be; for there is a capital defect in their very method of teaching. The books which they read are not well chosen; not so much as with regard to the language. Were even this circumstance duly considered, would Eutropius or Lucius Florius have any place among them: 'O, but I want to give a sketch of the Roman history.' And cannot you do this much better by English authors? Cannot you give the marrow of Roman history without ruining their style by bad Latin?"[4]

Yet another fault he had to find with the common method of language instruction: "In most schools little judgment is shown in the order of the books that are read. Some very difficult ones are read in the lower classes, 'Phaedrus's Fables' in particular; and some very easy ones are read long after, in utter defiance of common sense."[5]

In order to avoid these evils, Wesley himself chose the texts for class reading, and edited most of them anew. "In teaching the languages," he said, "care is taken to read those authors and those only, who join together the purity, the strength, and the elegance of their several tongues. In particular, no Roman author is read who lived later than the Augustan age. Only to these are added proper *Excerpta* from Juvenal, Persius, and Martial. To supply the place of bad Latin writers of antiquity, a few of the moderns are added. And indeed their writings are not unworthy of the Augustan age; being little inferior, either in purity or beauty of diction, to the best writers of that period."[6] Furthermore, he said, "We begin with the plainest of all; next read such as are a little more difficult, and gradually rise to those that are hardest of all."[7]

Kingswood students were not the only Methodists who stood in need of education. In addition to the articles in the *Arminian Magazine* on philosophy, natural history, physics, sociology, mythology, and the like, Wesley published a number of books for the instruction of his people at large.

In the field of history he published three. The *Short Roman History* (1773) was carefully prepared from *The Roman History, from the Building of Rome to the Ruin of the Commonwealth,* by Nathaniel Hooke.[8]

The principal sources of his *Concise History of England, from the Earliest Times to the Death of George II* (four volumes, 1776) were the histories of Goldsmith, Rapin, and Smollett.[9] According to his statement, he endeavored to lay great stress upon the important events, to pass lightly over those unimportant ones which had taken up so much space in earlier histories, to avoid the bias of partisan loyalties, and to point out the operation of God's providence in the events narrated. Taking Tacitus as his model, he strongly emphasized those incidents "which tend either to improve the understanding, or to inspire the heart with noble and generous sentiments."[10]

For a while Wesley's *Concise History* was held in high esteem. The profits from its sale enabled him to distribute £ 200 among the poor.[11] But he lacked the requisite training of the scholarly historian. As a history his book is of course utterly worthless today. It is, however, peculiarly interesting as it throws light on Wesley's independence of judgment. He was aware of his departure from the usual estimate of some characters. "I am sensible it must give offense," he said of his work, "as in many parts I am quite singular, particularly with regard to those greatly injured characters, Richard III and Mary Queen of Scots. But I must speak as I think, although still waiting for, and willing to receive better information."[12]

The material with which Wesley dealt when he compiled his *Concise Ecclesiastical History, from the Birth of Christ to the Beginning of the Present Century* was dry; and he knew it. He praised an earlier ecclesiastical historian in the highest terms he could find: "Much of his history is as lively as the nature of the subject will bear."[13] His own work was a sort of *cento,* made by the extraction of necessary material from two voluminous histories, one a translation from Dr. John Lawrence Mosheim of Gottingen and the other by Archdeacon Echard, of the Church of England.[14] In the interests of clarity he entirely omitted long sections that were "neither instructive nor entertaining;" and he made some attempt to simplify the prose of his predecessors: "Sallust, not Cicero, is the standard for the style of a history," he said, and corrected the fault which made history sound like oratory "by paring off the superfluity of words, and leaving only so many in every sentence, as sufficed to convey the meaning of it."[15]

He warned his readers of another characteristic of all ecclesiastical histories—one which he could not honestly remove from his own: "After all, there is one thing of which I judge it absolutely necessary to apprise the pious reader, (that he be not offended,) before he enters upon this or any other history of the church. Let him not expect to find a history of saints, of men that walked worthy of their high calling. It is true that there were a few in every age of these burning and shining lights. But they shone in a dark place, in a benighted world, a world full of darkness and cruel habitations."[16]

During the years of Wesley's life the opportunities for medical attention available to the poor were hopelessly and tragically inadequate. For a while he employed an apothecary, with whose assistance he maintained several free dispensaries. The good accomplished by this project was necessarily limited in its extent, and lack of funds finally made him abandon it. But by means of books he spread medical instruction among an enormous number of people.

According to his favorite custom, he published two abridgments of medical works. From a book by Dr. Tissot he extracted *Advices with respect to Health,* which, beginning in 1769, ran to eight editions;[17] and in his collected *Works* he printed *An Extract from Dr. Cadogan's Dissertation on the Gout and all Chronic Diseases.*

But Wesley also wrote several original treatises. His *Letter to a Friend concerning Tea* (1748) reflected one of those pet notions (in this case a prejudice against the "cup that cheers and not inebriates") which, not always wisely, he endeavored to impress upon other people. In *The Desideratum; or, Electricity made Plain and Useful* (1760) he attempted to summarize what had been learned about that mysterious force by Benjamin Franklin and others, and to inform his readers of its supposed medical properties.[18]

His most popular medical publications, however, were his books of prescriptions. In 1745 he published *A Collection of Receipts for the Use of the Poor,* a pamphlet that died after two editions. Since the lives of no persons are now likely to be affected by the little book, the nature of it may prove amusing. "I suppose there are very few infallible medicines," said Wesley in his advertisement; "but I believe those that follow will fail as seldom as any, and much more seldom than the costly ones in common use. From a vast number, I have selected those, which are not only *cheap* but safe: very few of them, if they do no good, being likely to do much harm. For most distempers I have set down several. If one does not help, another may. And they may generally be tried one (at some distance) after another, using the easiest and simplest first." His prescription for a headache was quaint: "Wear green hemlock that is tender, thickly spread on the soles of your feet. Shift it every day."[19]

Much more ambitious was *Primitive Physick; or an Easy and Natural Method of Curing Most Diseases.* The first edition appeared in 1747, and the successive editions, through the twenty-third (1791), were continually enlarged and revised.[20] From Wesley's day to ours, the *Primitive Physick* has elicited wide comment: commendation, condemnation, and mirth. The medical profession was almost as solidly and emphatically opposed to quackery in the eighteenth century as it is today; and some physicians considered Wesley's book dangerous. A certain Dr. William Hawes wrote a condemnatory review for *Lloyd's Evening Post,* and received a letter from Wesley which must have amused and angered him: "My bookseller informs me that since you published your remarks on the Primitive Physick, or a Natural and Easy Method of Curing most Disorders, there has been a greater demand for it than ever.

If, therefore, you would please to publish a few farther remarks, you would confer a farther favor upon Your humble servant—"[21]

Whatever may be said concerning the wisdom of Wesley's well-intentioned writing on how to cure diseases, his preface to *Primitive Physick,* advising people how to keep well, is far ahead of the usual thought of his time and full of sound recommendations that have not gone out of date. It is, moreover, wittily written.[22]

Wesley was interested in theoretical science as well as its practical application. The first three editions of his *Survey of the Wisdom of God in the Creation: or a Compendium of Natural Philosophy* represent three distinct versions. The two-volume edition of 1763 was basically an abridged translation of a Latin work by Professor Buddeaus, of the University of Jena, with notes written by Wesley and a number of other men.[23] The edition of 1770 was published in three volumes. The first two were practically identical with the first edition, and the third volume, a sort of appendix, contained additional material supplementary to the original chapters. In the edition of 1777 the contents of this third volume, further enlarged, were incorporated into the text. The whole work was swelled into five volumes by the addition of extracts from several other essays on natural philosophy.[24]

Wesley made no attempt to present a philosophical system for the phenomena of nature; the central theme which served to bring the described facts into some sort of harmony was his attribution of them all, with their interrelation, to the inscrutable wisdom of God. Its value lay in its record of the current opinions about nature.

Just before he was ready to send his third edition to the press, Wesley saw Oliver Goldsmith's recently published *History of the Earth and Animated Nature.* "I had not read over the first volume of this," he said, "when I almost repented of having wrote any thing on the head. It seemed to me, that had he published this but a few years sooner, my design would have been superseded; since the subject had fallen into the hands of one who had both greater abilities and more leisure for the work. It cannot be denied, that he is a fine writer. He was a person of strong judgment, of a lively imagination, and a master of language, both of the beauty and strength of the English tongue." Though Wesley found reason to go ahead with his publication—Goldsmith's book was objectionable on account of its great bulk and its consequent high price; and, Wesley thought, in accepting such stories as that of a sea-serpent which could raise itself out of the water higher than the main mast of a man-of-war, the author had displayed uncritical credulity—he borrowed from Goldsmith, here and there, material which he considered superior to what he had before intended to include.[25]

At the age of fifty years Wesley could hardly have foreseen in detail all the writing, abridging, and general editing he was yet to accomplish for the people whose betterment he took as his special province; but he had long been determined that they should be a reading people. In his original compositions he strove to employ only such words as would be familiar alike to the learned and the unlearned; but he well knew that in most stimulating books, even sometimes in his own, there were words whose occurrence would be a stumbling block to many Methodists. He set himself, therefore, to prepare such a book as would smooth the course; and in 1753 he published a dictionary.

In his remarks to the reader he for once let the edge of his wit go unsheathed. His title-page was startling: "*The Complete English Dictionary,* explaining most of those hard words which are to be found in the best English writers. By a Lover of Good English, and Common Sense. N. B. The author assures you, he thinks this is the best English Dictionary in the World."

In the preface outlining his purpose he again waxed humorous:

"As incredible as it may appear, I must allow, that this Dictionary is not published to get money; but to assist persons of common sense, and no learning, to understand the best English authors; and that with as little expense of either time or money as the nature of the thing will allow.

"To this end, it contains, not a heap of Greek and Latin words, just tagged with English terminations; (for no good English writer, none but vain and senseless pedants, give these any place in their writings;) not a scroll of barbarous law expressions, which are neither Greek, Latin, nor good English; not a crowd of technical terms, the meaning whereof is to be sought in books expressly wrote on the subjects to which they belong; not such English words as *and, of, but,* which stand so gravely in Mr. Bailey's, Pardon's, and Martin's Dictionaries; but 'most of those hard words which are found in the best English writers.' I say *most;* for I purposely omit, not only all that are not found in the best writers; not only all law words, and most technical terms; but likewise all the meaning of which may be easily gathered from those of the same derivation. And this I have done, in order to make this Dictionary both as short and cheap as possible.

"I should add no more, but that I have so often observed, the only way, according to the modern taste, for any author to procure commendation to his book, is, vehemently to commend it himself. For want of this deference to the public, several excellent tracts, lately printed, but left to commend themselves by their intrinsic worth, are utterly unknown or forgotten: whereas, if a writer of tolerable sense will but bestow a few violent encomiums on his own work; especially, if they are skilfully ranged in the title-page; it will pass through six editions in a trice: the world being too complaisant to give a gentleman the lie; and taking it for granted, he understands his own performance best.

"In compliance, therefore, with the taste of the age, I add that this little Dictionary is not only the shortest and cheapest, but likewise, by many degrees, the most correct, which is extant at this day. Many are the mistakes in all the other English Dictionaries which I have yet seen: whereas, I can truly say, I know of none in this: and I conceive the reader will believe me; for if I had, I should not have left it there. Use, then, this help, till you find a better."[26]

A better was not long in coming forth. Two years after Wesley's book first appeared, Dr. Samuel Johnson published his epoch-making *Dictionary.* Wesley's still had the advantages of shortness and cheapness; and in a brief statement appended to his original preface, Wesley informed the buyers of his second edition (1764) that he had "added some hundreds of words, which were omitted in the former: chiefly from Mr. Johnson's Dictionary, which I carefully looked over for that purpose."

To give a hint as to the sort of lexicographer Wesley was, here are fifteen words with their definitions, taken *verbatim et literatim* from his book. The first five and last five definitions in the volume are taken as typical. The other five in the list are religious words, whose definitions, coming from him, may prove interesting; it is to be noted that he does not define *God* or *predestination*. The apostrophes within the words are, as may be readily gathered, Wesley's method of indicating accent.

ABA'FT, behind, near the stern of a ship.

ABA'NDON, to give up, resign, forsake.

To ABA'SE, to bring low.

To ABA'SH, to make ashamed.

An A'BBOT, the chief of a convent.

The ZE'NITH, the point in the sky just over our heads.

ZE'PHYRUS, the west wind.

The ZO'DIAC, the space wherein all the planets perform their revolutions.

A ZONE, a girdle anciently worn by virgins.

The ZONES, the earth is divided into five, one torrid, two temperate, and two frigid.

DEISM, infidelity, denying the Bible.

CA'LVINISTS, they that hold absolute, unconditioned Predestination.

A ME'THODIST, one that lives according to the method laid down in the Bible.

PRESBYTE'RIANS, they who believe the ancient bishops and priests were of one and the same order.

The ELE'CT, all that truly believe in Christ.

CONCLUSION

JOHN WESLEY was personally responsible for three hundred and seventy-one separate publications. When it is recalled that one of these, *The Christian Library,* filled fifty volumes, that another, *The Arminian Magazine,* went through more than one hundred and fifty numbers while he was editor, and that it was a common occurrence for his separate books to run into upwards of a dozen editions each, one begins to realize what an enormous amount of printed matter he caused to be disseminated among English-speaking peoples.

The books we have examined comprise a good deal less than half of this large quantity. The scores of volumes which must be omitted from our consideration, however, were written more exclusively for definite religious purposes, and therefore fall under the classification of technical or professional literature. That is not to say that they were by any means all lacking in beauty. In editing the works of such men as Thomas à Kempis, Richard Baxter, William Law, and Jonathan Edwards, Wesley was bringing to greater popularity men of great force and charm; indeed much of his own writing, such as his *Earnest Appeal to Men of Reason and Religion,* is clothed in language of such dignity and power as to assure him a high rank among the masters of religious prose. And yet his devotional books, his admirable revision and notes on the New Testament, his doctrinal treatises, his controversial works, his short tracts, his editions of inspirational writings, and his own volumes defending, administering, and advising the Methodist Societies—all these, excellent as many of them are, have to do with a phase of Wesley's career which, repeatedly and ably treated in many a biography and history of Methodism, has not vitally concerned us in our review of his activities as a man of letters.

Wesley himself was as thoroughly indifferent to literary fame as he was to the financial rewards of his writings. Fame and money he used, indeed—fame to assist in the spread of his revival, and money to relieve the needs of the poor and assist in the support of his preachers—but as ends in themselves he despised both.[1] A single principle guided him in all things, "that of doing good to all men, of the ability that God giveth."[2]

Following that principle, he not only preached, organized religious societies, personally assisted the physical needs of the poor, and set in motion a force which was destined to change the whole aspect of English society; but also, as we have seen, he labored tirelessly and effectively to educate the poorer classes to the point where they might begin to enjoy the abundant pleasure and enlightening inspiration of great literature; he furnished an imposing body of poetry and prose for their consumption; and he made new and beautiful contributions to the literature of our tongue, both through the exercise of his own powers of composition and through the influential power of his personality.

With regard to his efforts to bring about a more intimate acquaintance between the great English multitudes and great English literature, he might well have modestly expressed the significance of his whole literary career with the statement and wish wherewith he closed his preface to Young's *Night Thoughts*: "I have made a little attempt, such as I could consistently with abundance of other employment. Let one that has more leisure and more abilities supply what is here wanting."

NOTES

Reference to works by Wesley is made by mention of the appropriate short title. Other books are usually designated by naming their authors. Full titles will be found in the bibliography.

CHAPTER ONE

1. Tyerman, II, 579.
2. *Ibid.,* III, 329.
3. *Ibid.,* III, 362.
4. Quoted in Edwards, p. 18.
5. *Letters,* VI, 290.
6. *Ibid.,* VI, 201.
7. *Ibid.,* I, 54.
8. *Ibid.,* VI, 129.
9. *Ibid.,* VII, 81.

CHAPTER TWO

1. *Journal,* I, 83.
2. *Ibid.,* I, 84.
3. *Ibid.,* I, 193.
4. *Ibid.,* I, 194.
5. *"An Extract of the Rev. Mr. John Wesley's Journal,* from his embarking for Georgia to his return to London. . . . Bristol: Printed for S. and F. Farley." There is no date, but Green is undoubtedly right in placing it in 1738 or 1739. See his *Bibliography,* pp. 14-15.

   For Wesley's statement of his reasons for publishing this *Journal Extract* see *Journal,* I, 84-85.
6. *Journal,* I, 87-102.
7. *"An Extract of the Rev. Mr. John Wesley's Journal,* from February 1, 1737-38, to his Return from Germany. . . . London: printed by W. Strahan; . . . 1740." See Green's Bibliography, p. 16. All the contemporary editions of the *Journal Extracts* are described in detail by Green, *q. v.*
8. *Journal,* I, 429.
9. *Ibid.,* II, 67.
10. *Idem.*
11. *Ibid.,* III, 507.
12. Wesley Historical Society *Publications,* I, 16.
13. The new material Curnock indicated by unobtrusive enclosure in square brackets. His basic text was the printed *Journal Extracts.* In addition to correcting ascertainable errors, he says in his Preface, "Here and there—very occasionally—a more vigorous or picturesque phrase, borrowed from another copy in Wesley's handwriting, has been substituted for the printed version of the same sentence." See *Journal,* I, vi. It may be added that variants from this eclectic text have not been included in the edition, even in footnotes.
14. *Journal,* Curnock's Introduction, I, 41.
15. Tyerman, III, 616, footnote.

CHAPTER THREE

1. See Southey, II, 340.
2. *Letters,* IV, 256.
3. *Ibid.,* IV, 72.
4. *Ibid.,* I, 4.
5. *Ibid.,* VII, 182.
6. *Ibid.,* VIII, 125.
7. *Ibid.,* I, xvi.
8. *Ibid.,* VI, 18, 166, 308; VII, 258, 306; VIII, 190, etc.
9. *Ibid.,* VI, 160-64.
10. *Ibid.,* III, 165.
11. *Ibid.,* VIII, 265.
12. *Ibid.,* IV, 232, 256-58, 266-68.

CHAPTER FOUR

1. *Letters,* II, 152.
2. See Green's *Bibliography* for full bibliographical data.
3. *Journal,* IV, 48.
4. *Idem.*
5. Moore, II, 360-61.
6. "Some Remarks on Mr. Hill's 'Review of All the Doctrines Taught by Mr. John Wesley,'" *Works,* VI, 149.
7. *Letters,* IV, 207.
8. *Idem.*
9. "Remarks on Mr. Hill's 'Review . . . ,'" *Works,* VI, 149.
10. Green has suggested that Wesley's first design in publishing the *Library* was solely to furnish his preachers a convenient body of divinity. But even though this conjecture is probably accurate, Wesley shortly broadened the scope of his aim. See Green's *Bibliography,* p. 95.
11. See *Christian Library,* I, vi.
12. *Ibid.,* I, vii.
13. *Idem.*
14. *Ibid.,* I, vii-viii.
15. *Ibid.,* I, viii.
16. *Idem.*
17. *Ibid.,* I, ix.
18. *Idem.*
19. *Letters,* IV, 122.
20. *Ibid.,* IV, 121.
21. *Christian Library,* I, iv.
22. *Ibid.,* II, 3.

    A curious extension of Wesley's purpose that the *Library* should show the practical workings of Christianity may be seen in volume XXII. There he prints a treatise called "Directions for Married Persons: Describing the Duties common to both, and peculiar to each of them," by William Whateley. It was a subject upon which Wesley himself might profitably have received some really sound advice.

CHAPTER FIVE

1. See G. C. Cell's chapter on this subject in *The Rediscovery of John Wesley,* New York, 1935.
2. *Arminian Magazine,* I, iv.
3. *Letters,* VI, 295.

4. *Idem.*
5. *Arminian Magazine,* I, vi-vii.
6. Archbishop Usher, Volume II; and Armelle Nicholas, Volume III.
7. Telford, p. 327.
8. *Letters,* VII, 48. This statement appeared first in the *Arminian Magazine* itself.
9. John Dennis, *The Grounds of Criticism in Poetry,* London, 1704; and *Arminian Magazine,* I, 39-40. It seems highly probable that Wesley had read Dennis' essay.
10. *Arminian Magazine,* III, iv-v.
11. The actual details of business and distribution he had caused to devolve upon the "Book Room Stewards," a group which he had organized for this express purpose. See Simon, J. S., *John Wesley and the Advance of Methodism,* pp. 232-33.
12. Southey, II, 232.
13. *Arminian Magazine,* IX, 462-63.
14. *Ibid.,* preface to volume VII.
15. Hampson, III, 154-55.
16. Martin, Edward, "Sale of Wesley's Publications," Wesley Historical Society *Proceedings,* I, 90.

CHAPTER SIX

1. Whitehead, I, 235.
2. *Letters,* I, 8-9.
3. *Ibid.,* I, 27-28.
4. *Ibid.,* I, 28.
5. Whitehead, I, 251.
6. *Ibid.,* I, 249. The paraphrase was first published in *The Arminian Magazine,* volume I.
7. *Journal,* I, 110.
8. *Ibid.,* I, 112; and *passim* through volume I.
9. Hatfield, James Taft, "John Wesley's Translations of German Hymns," *P M L A,* XI, 180. I am heavily indebted to this article, which runs from page 171 to page 199 in the *Publications* for 1896. Because I have not, as Wesley would say, followed him for better, for worse, I do not shift responsibility to him for aught but the statements of fact which he has certified. Professor Hatfield identified twenty-nine translations with their originals, and drew sound conclusions from a very careful comparison.

   In 1798 the Wesley Historical Society *Proceedings,* I, 48-49, contained a list of the German translations, compiled by C. D. Hardcastle. One hymn mentioned by Professor Hatfield does not appear; but the list contains two hymns, first printed in *Psalms and Hymns,* 1741, (see Green's *Bibliography,* p. 20) which Professor Hatfield did not have in his enumeration. It is possible that Professor Hatfield was not able to have access to the 1741 publication, for he does not mention it at all.

   The results of an exhaustive count of the German translations is to be found in a little book by Henry Bett, *The Hymns of Methodism,* 1920, pp. 110-12. According to this list, there are extant thirty-three such hymns by John Wesley, one of which was never published in his lifetime. Bett makes the interesting point that the sources for all but one of the published hymns were in *Das Gesangbuch der Gemeinde in Herrnhuth,* published in 1735, which was the Moravian hymnal used in Georgia while Wesley was there.

There is enough fresh material on the German hymns to make Bett's book a valuable and interesting supplement to Professor Hatfield's article.

10. *Journal,* I, 229, Curnock's note.
11. *Ibid.,* I, 425.
12. From Sermon on "Knowing Christ after the Flesh," *Works,* II, 443.
13. However, see Hatfield, pp. 185-86. Professor Hatfield emphasizes Wesley's correctness: "Considering the fact that German studies hardly existed in England at the time, it is remarkable that we can say of Wesley (what perhaps could not be said of Scott or Coleridge) that he never shows a flagrant misunderstanding of the text." But, continues Professor Hatfield, "In sparse cases mistakes seem to have occurred;" and he proceeds to list the possible errors. It seems to me that Wesley's free use of the original renders it quite probable that even in these cases he was deliberately changing the sense.

For example, Hatfield notices that

> und lass biss in den tod
> uns allzeit deiner pflege
> und treu *empfohlen seyn*—

appears in Wesley's translation as

> Let us in Life, in Death,
> Thy steadfast truth declare,
> And *publish* with our latest Breath
> Thy Love and Guardian Care!

It is impossible absolutely to deny that Wesley misunderstood the meaning of *empfehlen.* Nevertheless I am inclined to believe that he transformed the stanza consciously. It is a minor point, no doubt; but I shall give my reasons.

1. Wesley had absolutely no scruple against making any change he saw fit.

2. Evangelist of evangelists, he was convinced of the duty of a Christian to bear witness to the grace of God.

3. He was particularly fond of having the testimony of dying Christians. I have already called attention to his boast, "Our people die well." Witness the numerous accounts in *The Arminian Magazine* which tell of Methodists publishing with their latest breath God's love and guardian care. Witness, finally, his own desire that his last words should be words of praise, and his insistence as he died that "The best of all is, God is with us."

In the light, therefore, of the strong probability that Wesley had a definite purpose in rendering the hymn as he did, and in view of the fact that *empfehlen* is a common, easy word, used in a perfectly normal, easy construction, it seems only natural to conclude that this is a case, not of error, but of deliberate change.

I believe a similar course of argument could be successfully brought to bear upon the other instances of possible error which Professor Hatfield lists. It is enough, however, to enter a *caveat* against the assumption that where Wesley differs from his original he does so simply through error.

14. Professor Hatfield gives the following illustration to show that "Wesley can be extremely literal."

See his article, p. 185.

In hoffnung kan ich frölich sagen:
Gott hat der Höllen macht geschlagen,
Gott führt mich aus dem kampf und streit
In seine ruh und sicherheit.

Already springing Hope I feel;
God will destroy the Power of Hell;
God from the Land of Wars and Pain
Leads me where Peace and Safety reign.

15. See, for example, *Letters,* IV, 194.
16. From Sermon on "Knowing Christ after the Flesh," *Works,* II, 443.
17. It was partially because of his contempt for their indecent imagery that Wesley published his stinging rebuke of Count Zinzendorf's hymns. He simply collected a group of the Moravian leader's worst effusions, and printed them with an ironic preface in a pamphlet having this title-page: *"Hymns Composed for the use of the Brethren.* By the Right Reverend and Most Illustrious C. Z. Published for the Benefit of all Mankind, in the year 1749." See Green's *Bibliography,* pp. 65-66; and cf. *Journal,* III, 389.
18. From Sermon on "Knowing Christ after the Flesh," *Works,* II, 444.
19. This statement applies to the hymns which were translated from a single original. Some of Wesley's German hymns are centos. One, for instance, derives from four sources. For all such detailed information Professor Hatfield's article is a reliable guide.
20. Professor Hatfield (see his article, p. 181) has made a classification of Wesley's stanza forms. It is significant that twenty-four out of the twenty-nine hymns he deals with are in stanzas of four iambic tetrameter lines, or, as the pattern is usually called, long meter.
21. *A Collection of Hymns, for the Use of the People called Methodists,* 1780, preface.
22. Hatfield, p. 186.
23. See Hatfield, p. 187, for numerous other examples. In this connection I find myself impelled to make one other adverse criticism of a detail in Professor Hatfield's excellent paper. He says (p. 184-85), "Of mixed metaphors Wesley has a decided dislike, as in the stanza . . . where the believer is likened both to a lamb and a lion, or [in the line]:

    da solst du mein lamm, mein licht und tempel seyn."

    But a little later (p. 187) it is pointed out in another connection that the German

    mir, dem schatten,

    is rendered in Wesley's English version thus:

    In Sin conceiv'd, of Woman born,
    A Worm, a Leaf, a Blast, a Shade.

    Wherein "mein lamm, mein licht und tempel" is rhetorically different from "A Worm, a Leaf, a Blast, a Shade" does not easily appear.
24. For these two and other examples of Wesley's bold manner for the heightening of his effects, see Hatfield, pp. 188-91.
25. In the preface to his *Poetical Fragments,* London, 1681; quoted in the introduction to *The Works of George Herbert,* London, 1859, II, vi.
26. In his *Life of Dr. John Donne;* Walton's *Lives,* London, 1845, p. 63.
27. I have followed Curnock's count. See his footnote: *Journal,* I, 242.

28. G. Osborn, in *The Poetical Works of John and Charles Wesley,* Advertisement, VIII, xv, says that "the two brothers . . . agreed not to distinguish their hymns," and that "Mr. Bradburn received this statement from Mr. J. Wesley." Osborn continues: "any distinction now attempted must be to a great extent, if not wholly, conjectural. But [the editor] hopes to be excused for observing that his own inquiries have led him to think it likely that Mr. John Wesley contributed more largely to these joint publications than is commonly supposed; and that the habit of attributing almost everything found in them to his brother is scarcely consistent with a due regard to accuracy."

In some cases the possibility of John's authorship can be definitely eliminated, as when a volume was published under Charles's name alone.

29. Proof is readily available. There has been no doubt about the translations from the Latin, or the paraphrase of the 104th Psalm.

Conclusive proof that the German translations are John Wesley's is assembled in Professor Hatfield's article in *P M L A, q. v.*

The Rev. Nehemiah Curnock, in his edition of John Wesley's *Journal,* has given the facts that irresistibly point to John as the adapter of George Herbert's poetry.

The Rev. John Telford made the determination in regard to the paraphrase of the Lord's prayer; see his *Life of John Wesley,* p. 222.

Telford is also among those who have shown John Wesley to be the translator of the Spanish hymn; see his *Methodist Hymn-Book Illustrated,* p. 269.

The translation from the French is the only poem about which the proof is at all doubtful. For a careful and cautious review of the evidence see Henry Bett, *The Hymns of Methodism,* pp. 62-64. There is a possibility that the hymn may have been translated by Dr. Byrom and merely revised by Wesley. A majority of those who have studied the question ascribe the translation solely to the latter.

The most ambitious attempt to separate the original hymns of John Wesley from those of his brother will be found in Bett's *Hymns of Methodism,* Appendix IV, pp. 129-35. He names nine hymns which he thinks are certainly John's, and lays down a series of test-principles which may be applied to a suspected hymn. All his principles are based on internal evidence. It is unnecessary here to point out how peculiarly inadequate such evidence must be in the case of a man almost all of whose positively identifiable poetry is translation. Bett's discussion, however, is suggestive and sympathetic, and may be valuable to those who do not require conclusive proof of authorship.

A letter from the Rev. John Telford written some months before his lamented death assured me that he believed, as I do, that the only entirely original poem definitely attributable to John Wesley is that on Grace Murray. See immediately below.

30. The whole poem is printed in Dr. Augustine Leger's interesting book, *Wesley's Last Love,* pp. 98-105, and also in Henry Moore's *Life of Wesley,* II, 171. Wesley, of course, never published the piece. It lay practically unknown until Dr. Leger reproduced it, *verbatim et literatim,* in 1910, from a diary of Wesley's which he found in the British Museum.

CHAPTER SEVEN

1. *Letters,* VI, 283.
2. Sermon on "Knowing Christ after the Flesh," *Works,* II, 444.
3. *A Plain Account of Christian Perfection,* Fourth Edition, 1777. See *Works,* VI, 499.

4. Witness the irregular stanzas in his paraphrase of Psalm CIV. See Whitehead, I, 249 ff., or *Arminian Magazine,* Volume I.
5. See Burgess, p. 68.
6. Benson, p. 220.
7. From Preface to *A Collection of Hymns, for the Use of the People Called Methodists,* 1780.
8. Burgess, p. 75, and the hymnals, for example, of the Methodist Episcopal and the Presbyterian church.
9. From Preface to *A Collection of Hymns, for the Use of the People called Methodists,* 1780.
10. *Idem.*
11. Life and Letters of James Martineau, New York, 1902, II, 99.
12. The two editions I have examined are the second, 1754, and the fourteenth, 1768; but Green's *Bibliography* indicates that the same preface appeared in the first edition and was retained in all. See also *Works,* VII, 604.
13. Benson, p. 255, amplifies and illustrates this statement.
14. The Wesley family, however, did boast some notable musicians with creative ability. Charles Wesley's two sons, Samuel and Charles, and his grandson Samuel Sebastian Wesley all had distinguished careers in music; and all composed hymn tunes.
15. See Green's *Bibliography,* p. 24. *Hymns and Sacred Poems* was published in three volumes, in 1739, 1740, and 1742.
16. Lightwood, James T., "Notes on the Foundery Tune-Book," Wesley Historical Society *Proceedings,* II, 160.
17. Wiseman, "John Wesley's Tunes," in *Wesley Studies,* p. 167.
18. *Idem.*
19. Preface to *Select Hymns,* etc., 1765. See also *Works,* VII, 602.
20. *Idem.*
21. *Idem.*
22. *Sacred Melody,* the last page (unnumbered). This is at the head of the "Directions for Congregational Singing."
23. This was issued also separately, in pamphlet form. See Green's *Bibliography,* pp. 118-19.
24. The date of this publication has not been confidently fixed. Green believes 1781. See his *Bibliography,* pp. 214-15.
25. Wiseman, pp. 163-64.
26. *Ibid.,* pp. 164-65.
27. *Ibid.,* p. 167.
28. Benson, p. 240.
29. See also *Works,* VII, 609.
30. Preface to *A Collection of Hymns, for the Use of the People called Methodists,* 1780. See also his heated reply to a contemptuous reference to the Methodist Hymns by the Monthly Reviewers: *Letters,* III, 196-99.
31. Minutes of the Conference of 1746. See Wesley Historical Society *Publications,* Number I, 1896, p. 32.
32. *Minutes of the Methodist Conferences,* I, 80.
33. Wiseman, p. 168.
34. *Journal,* V, 290.
35. *Ibid.,* VI, 61.

CHAPTER EIGHT

1. See *Letters,* I, 104; IV, 247 f.; V, 220, 286; VII, 81 f.
2. *Moral and Sacred Poems,* Dedication.
3. *Idem.*

4. *Idem.*
5. Such as John Gambold, a preacher for whose compositions the editor had a great fondness, and the Wesleys—Samuel (senior and junior), Charles, and John himself.
6. *Letters,* II, 27.
7. See Green's *Bibliography,* p. 33.
8. *Journal,* I, 47 and 65-66; Curnock's Introduction.
9. Tyerman, I, 499.
10. *An Extract from Milton's Paradise Lost,* prefatory address "To the Reader." See also *Works,* VII, 601.
11. *Idem.*
12. *Idem.*
13. *Idem.*
14. The following table will show the even distribution of deletions by books. The numbers indicate the total number of lines per book.

Books	Wesley's Edition	Original
I	576	798
II	896	1055
III	562	742
IV	884	1015
V	693	907
VI	798	912
VII	562	640
VIII	561	653
IX	953	1189
X	889	1104
XI	799	901
XII	535	649
Totals	8708	10565

Number of lines deleted—1857. This is 17.5% of the original.

15. Milton, *Paradise Lost,* i, 406-11.
16. *Ibid.,* i, 768-76.
17. *Ibid.,* i, 645-49.
18. *Ibid.,* i, 214-20.
19. *Ibid.,* i, 439 and 446.
20. *Ibid.,* i, 476.
21. As "*Adamantine*—Firm like Diamond" and "*Warping*—working themselves forward. A sea-term."

    These and the other examples in the paragraph referred to are taken from the notes to Book i.
22. As "*The Tuscan Artist*—Galileo, a native of Tuscany" and "*Old Euphrates*—Mentioned by the oldest historian, in the earliest account of Time. It was the Eastern boundary of Canaan."
23. In *Le poète Edward Young,* p. 499.
24. *An Extract from Dr. Young's Night Thoughts on Life, Death, and Immortality,* prefatory address "To the Reader." See also *Works,* VII, 602-03.
25. *Journal,* V, 296.
26. *An Extract from Night Thoughts,* prefatory address "To the Reader." See also *Works,* VII, 602-03.
27. *Idem.* The notes were grouped at the end of the Night to which they refer.
28. *Idem.*
29. *Ibid.,* p. 23.
30. *Ibid.,* p. 111.

31. *Ibid.*, prefatory address "To the Reader."

A second edition of Wesley's *Extract* appeared in 1794. An unabridged edition of the *Night Thoughts,* with Wesley's notes, along with Young's poem *The Last Day,* was published in 1840; and a volume with similar contents came out in 1863. See Green's *Bibliography,* p. 153.

32. *The Works of George Herbert,* II, vii, note.
33. See, for example, *Letters,* I, 42, 66, 169; II, 205; III, 45; VII, 163, 170.
34. *Bibliography,* p. 171.

CHAPTER NINE

1. Bunyan, p. 146.
2. Wesley's abridgment, p. 5.
3. Bunyan, pp. 206-09.
4. According to Wesley's Faithful, the Grace of God manifests itself to the Christian thus:

(1.) He is convinced of sin. (2.) He receiveth Redemption in Christ's blood. (3.) Being justified by Faith, he hath the Peace of God, which passeth all understanding. (4.) He rejoiceth (a.) in the Hope of the Glory of God, (b.) that he hath now received the Atonement, the Spirit of God bearing witness with his spirit that he is a Child of God. (5.) The Love of God is shed abroad in his Heart, by the Holy Ghost which is given unto him. (6.) He keepeth the Commandments and sinneth not.

5. Bunyan, pp. 188-89.
6. Green's *Bibliography,* p. 28, note.
7. *Idem.*
8. Quoted in Tyerman, III, 172-73.
9. *Henry, Earl of Moreland,* Wesley's address "To the Reader." For the full title of Wesley's version see bibliography.
10. This gentleman was a devoted member of a Methodist society in Dublin.
11. *Letters,* VI, 96.
12. See *Arminian Magazine,* X, 160-61.
13. *Henry, Earl of Moreland,* Wesley's address "To the Reader."
14. There are about 219,000 words in *Henry, Earl of Moreland,* and about 318,000 in *The Fool of Quality.*
15. *Henry, Earl of Moreland,* Wesley's address "To the Reader."
16. For example, Wesley deleted the following passages. (The references here and throughout this section are made to the original *Fool of Quality.* For the edition used, see bibliography.)

II, 170-84: a long controversial tirade, in dialogue, against the slowness and inefficiency of the courts;

III, 237-52: a few illustrative incidents and then a long conversation on the political and social philosophy of personal financial debt;

IV, 88-127: a conversation in which the topic under discussion varies from the law of love in the human heart, through divers religious matters, to the history and nature of British liberty and the nature of the British Constitution.

17. Brooke, I, 55.
18. *Ibid.*, I, 122.
19. *Ibid.*, IV, 14.
20. *Ibid.*, I, 210-11.
21. Among the stories omitted are these, which appear in the original.

II, 147-52: a long story of the events connected with a Mr. Snarle's haunted house;

II, 212-21: two stories illustrative of the dual nature of man's heart: Jacob and Esau struggling against each other in the womb of their mother Rebecca, and the history of Cyrus, Penthea, and Araspes;

II, 232-75: the account of a reception held at the home of Lady Maitland;

III, 124-35: an account of the wandering life with Gypsies; this story is part of the long narrative of the "reprobate," one of the many incidental characters.

22. Brooke, I, 98.
23. *Ibid.*, I, 213.
24. In his *John Wesley,* London: Macmillan, 1927.
25. Hutton, W. H., *John Wesley,* pp. 165-66.

    Mr. Hutton continues: "He suppressed the one and thus exaggerated the other: he removed the balance, which indeed had a certain literary art in it; and the result is to make the book, as he presented it, tedious to the very limit of the unbearable." He goes on to say of Wesley, in this connection: "Sometimes as a judge of literature he seemed to know no more than an idiot or a child of fourteen." That conclusion is as unsound in its critical judgment as it is pert in phraseology. Here is another of Mr. Hutton's reasons for objecting to Wesley's treatment of *The Fool of Quality*: "In the original the crowd of exciting incident is interspersed with philosophic dialogue and reflection. Both are tedious, but when they are so near together they modify each other." If Mr. Hutton's critical taste were universally shared, of course, Wesley's work would have been a failure. I, for one, heartily disagree.
26. Pages 37-49. Here the Earl outlines a scheme of his: by building a great inland-waterways system the government could provide work for all the idle men in England and make for the future prosperity of the nation.
27. Green's *Bibliography* (p. 209) mentions six, and I have seen one more not listed there: Plymouth: J. Bennett, 1816.
28. Tyerman, III, 342.
29. *Letters,* VI, 228. *The History of the Human Heart* was the subtitle of *Juliet Grenville.*
30. Everett's *Life of Clark;* quoted in Tyerman, III, 342.
31. Stephen, Leslie, *English Literature and Society in the Eigheenth Century,* London, 1907, p. 149.
32. *Life of Fletcher,* pp. 162-63. See also *Works,* VI, 468.
33. Here is a list of persons whose Lives Wesley edited and published: Halyburton, DeRenty, John Nelson, Samuel Hitchens, Thomas Hitchens, Thomas Hogg, Matthew Lee, John Janeway, Richard More, Nathanael Othen, Thomas Walsh, David Brainerd, Mary Langson, Ann Rogers, Eliza Jackson, John Dillon, Ann Johnson, Nicholas Mooney, Alice Gilbert, Madame Guion, Gregory Lopez, Elizabeth Hindmarsh, Thomas Mitchell, John Haime, Silas Todd, Jane Newland.

    There were three journals: by Mary Gilbert, Elizabeth Harper, and John Nelson; and three compilations of letters: by Jane Cooper, Joseph Alleine, and Mrs. Lefevre.

    A description of each of these publications may be found in Green's *Bibliography.*
34. *Letters,* V, 340.
35. Some of the correspondence relating to the accumulation of information about incidents and facts may be found in *Letters,* VII, 297, 307, 312, 328, and 338.
36. See *Letters,* VII, 341; and cf. *Letters,* VI, 356.
37. *Life of Fletcher,* prefatory address "To the Reader."
38. *Ibid.,* pp. 14-15. See also *Works,* VI, 429-30.
39. *Ibid.,* pp. 199-200. See also *Works,* VI, 477.

CHAPTER TEN

1. See *Works*, VI, 346. Here Wesley proposes and answers the question: "How Far is it the Duty of a Christian Minister to Preach Politics?"
2. Discussion of these facts may be found in the following illuminating books:

   Thompson, D. D., *John Wesley as a Social Reformer*, New York: Eaton and Mains, 1898.

   Warner, W. J., *The Wesleyan Movement in the Industrial Revolution*, New York: Longmans, 1930.

   Edwards, Maldwyn, *John Wesley and the Eighteenth Century*, New York: The Abingdon Press, 1933.
3. *Works*, VI, 278.
4. *Journal*, V, 445-46.
5. Edwards, p. 118. For an intelligent discussion of Wesley's whole relationship with the Abolition movement, see Edwards' Chapter VIII.
6. For fuller descriptions of these pamphlets see Green's *Bibliography*, p. 159. For a discussion of the political theories Wesley held, see Edwards' Chapter II.
7. Under the date April 4, 1776, Wesley wrote in his journal: "I began an answer to that dangerous tract, Dr. Price's Observations on Liberty, which, if practiced, would overturn all government and bring in universal anarchy." See *Journal*, VI, 100.
8. *Works*, VI, 311. Mr. Maldwyn Edwards says (p. 31): "The logic of his statement compelled him to say that the greatest liberty is under a despot. This he refused to admit." This sort of logical extension is one which Wesley himself was not averse to using. Even so it is not quite fair. In the present instance Wesley was not calling upon deductive reasoning but the empirical results of historical observation. On these grounds, of course, he may well be combatted.
9. *A Calm Address to our American Colonies*, 1775.
   A Seasonable Address to the More Serious Part of the Inhabitants of Great Britain, respecting the unhappy Contest between us and our American Brethren: With an Occasional Word Interspersed to those of a Different Complexion, 1776.
   A Calm Address to the Inhabitants of England, 1777.
10. *A Serious Address to the People of England, with regard to the State of the Nation.*
11. *A Compassionate Address to the Inhabitants of Ireland.*
12. *An Account of the Conduct of the War in the Middle Colonies. Extracted from a Late Author*, 1780.

    An Extract from a Reply to the Observations of Lieut. Gen. Sir William Howe, on a Pamphlet entitled, Letters to a Nobleman, 1781.

    *An Extract of a Letter to the Right Honourable Lord Viscount H**e on his Naval Conduct in the American War*, 1781.

    These publications are further described in Green's *Bibliography*: the first on p. 201, and the last two on p. 210.
13. *A Calm Address to our American Colonies*, 2nd Edition, prefatory address "To the Reader." See also *Works*, VI, 293.
14. See his *Free Thoughts on the Present State of Public Affairs*, 1770.
15. See *Letters*, VI, 155-60 (To Lord Dartmouth), and 160-64 (To Lord North). These letters contain an able and eloquent appeal for a conciliatory policy towards America.
16. *A Calm Address to our American Colonies*, 2nd Edition, 1775, prefatory address "To the Reader." See also *Works*, VI, 293.

17. Southey (II, 283) says: "Mr. Wesley afterwards perceived that the class of persons whom he had here supposed to be the prime movers of this unhappy contest, were only aiders and abettors, and that the crisis had come on from natural causes."
18. I have here described the "New Edition corrected and enlarged." I have not seen the first edition; but apparently what I have said would apply, in general, to it also. See Green's *Bibliography,* pp. 180-81.
19. *A Calm Address to the Inhabitants of England.* See also *Works,* VI, 328-36.
20. Southey, II, 244.
21. *Ibid.,* II, 244-45.

    That other circumstances, however, contributed to the American distaste for Methodists is illustrated in a contemporary letter, written by one Samuel Purviance, Jr., and dated Baltimore, May 4, 1777. Primarily concerned with narrating the suspicious actions of one Captain Web, a Methodist preacher believed to be a spy, it reads, in part, as follows: "It is a certain truth that all the Denomination called Methodists allmost to a Man (with us) are Enemies to our Cause under the Mask of Religion, and are countenanced by the Tories—One of their Preachers did lately in this place tell his Hearers that every Man killed in Battle woud certainly go to Hell. Can the worst avowed Tories propagate a more dangerous doctrine to weak Minds."

    A true copy of this autograph letter, which is in possession of Judge H. E. Pickersgill, of Perth Amboy, New Jersey, I was enabled to see by the kindness of Dr. Charles Leonard Lundin, professor of history in the University of Indiana.
22. *Letters,* VI, 182.
23. *A Calm Address to the Inhabitants of England.* See also *Works,* VI, 328.
24. Trevelyan, III, 267-68.
25. Tyerman, III, 191.
26. Quoted in Moore, II, 360.
27. Winchester, 231-32.
28. This preface was in large part an answer to a pamphlet by the Rev. Caleb Evans, a Baptist minister at Bristol: *A Letter to the Rev. Mr. John Wesley, occasioned by his "Calm Address."* It was an able attack. Though Wesley assumes a scornful tone, the thrust cut home enough to elicit a strenuous reply.

    See Tyerman, III, 187-88.
29. Tyerman, III, 191.
30. Trevelyan, III, 270.
31. *Letters,* VI, 192.
32. *Ibid.,* VI, 192-93.
33. *Journal,* VI, 82-83.
34. *Letters,* VI, 182.
35. Lecky, II, 630-31.

    In a footnote Lecky makes an error. He says: "It is remarkable that Wesley never makes the slightest acknowledgment of his obligation to *Taxation no Tyranny* of Johnson." As we have seen, this is not true.

CHAPTER ELEVEN

1. On October 15, 1750, for example, he said, "I read over Holmes' *Latin Grammar* and extracted from it what was needful to perfect our own." See *Journal,* III, 499.

2. *Letters,* I, 192.
3. See "A Plain Account of Kingswood School," *Arminian Magazine,* IV, 487.
4. *Ibid.,* IV, 384.
5. *Idem.*
6. *Ibid.,* IV, 486.
7. Here is a list of the Latin texts he edited for Kingswood School:
   Praelectiones Pueriles
   Mathurini Corderii Colloquia Selecta
   Historiae et Praecepta Selecta
   Thomae a Kempis de Christo Imitando
   Cornelii Nepotis Excellentium Imperatorum Vitae
   Desiderii Erasmi Roterodami Colloquia Selecta
   Caii Sallustii Crispi Bellum Catilinarum et Jugurthinum
   Phaedri Fabulae Selectae
   Selecta ex Ovidio, Virgilio, Horatio, Juvenale, Martiale, Persio.
   Latin authors in use at Kingswood besides these were: Caesar, Terence, Valleius Paterculus, Bengelius, Tully, and Virgil.
8. "A copy of the 4th ed. of this Hooke's history (London, Tonson, &c.), is in the Richmond College Library, with Wesley's abridgments marked throughout, as though he had prepared it for publication or for use in Kingswood School." (Green's *Bibliography,* p. 168.)
9. See *Concise History of England,* preface, I, vi-vii. See also *Works,* VII, 560.
10. *Ibid., passim.*
11. See Green's *Bibliography,* pp. 185-86.
12. *Journal,* VI, 96.
13. *Concise Ecclesiastical History,* preface, p. iv. See also *Works,* VII, 576.
14. *Idem.*
15. *Ibid.,* p. vii. See also *Works,* VII, 577.
16. *Ibid.,* pp. vii-viii. See also *Works,* VII, 577-78.
17. See Green's *Bibliography,* p. 145.
18. Wesley bought four electrical machines for the use of poor people. I have heard that one of these is still in existence.
19. I quote this from Green's *Bibliography,* p. 39. I have not been able to lay hands on the original pamphlet.
20. A thirty-second edition appeared in 1828. See Green's *Bibliography,* p. 50.
21. *Letters,* VI, 225-26.
22. This pleasant little essay may be found in *Works,* VII, 583-91.
23. Green's *Bibliography,* p. 125.
24. Chiefly Bonnet's *The Contemplation of Nature,* and Duten's *Enquiry into the Origin of the Discoveries Attributed to the Moderns.* See Green's *Bibliography,* pp. 191-92.
25. See *Survey of the Wisdom of God in the Creation,* third edition, preface, pp. ix-x. See also *Works,* VII, 579-80.
26. This preface appears also in *Works,* VII, 553-54.

CONCLUSION

1. And yet he might have become wealthy from the earnings of his pen. From profits derived from the sale of his books—and it must be remembered that he sold them as cheaply as possible—he was enabled to give away during his life well above the equivalent of $100,000. See Tyerman, III, 616.
2. *Letters,* IV, 121.

BIBLIOGRAPHY

Benson, Louis F., THE ENGLISH HYMN, ITS DEVELOPMENT AND USE IN WORSHIP
Philadelphia: The Presbyterian Board of Publication, 1915.

Bett, Henry, THE HYMNS OF METHODISM IN THEIR LITERARY RELATIONS
London: The Epworth Press, New Edition, 1920.

Brooke, Henry, THE FOOL OF QUALITY: or, The History of Henry Earl of Moreland
In five volumes
London: W. Johnston, 1766-70.

Bunyan, John, THE PILGRIM'S PROGRESS
The text edited by John Brown, D. D.
Cambridge: at the University Press, 1907.

Burgess, William Pennington, WESLEYAN HYMNOLOGY
London: John Snow, 1846.

Cell, George Croft, THE REDISCOVERY OF JOHN WESLEY
New York: The Abingdon Press, 1935.

Dennis, John, THE GROUNDS OF CRITICISM IN POETRY
London: 1704.

Edwards, Maldwyn, JOHN WESLEY AND THE EIGHTEENTH CENTURY
A Study of his Social and Political Influence
New York: The Abingdon Press, 1933.

Elton, Oliver, A SURVEY OF ENGLISH LITERATURE, 1730-80
In two volumes
New York: The Macmillan Company, 1928.

Emory, John, (Editor) THE WORKS OF THE REV. JOHN WESLEY, A. M.
New York: Carlton and Porter, 1856.

Green, Richard, THE WORKS OF JOHN AND CHARLES WESLEY
A Bibliography
London: Methodist Publishing House, 1906.

Hampson, John, MEMOIRS OF THE LATE REV. JOHN WESLEY, A. M.
In three volumes
London: Printed for the Author, 1791.

Hatfield, James Taft, "John Wesley's Translations of German Hymns"
Publications of the Modern Language Association, vol. XI.

THE WORKS OF GEORGE HERBERT IN PROSE AND VERSE.
In two volumes
London: Bell and Daldy, 1859.

Hutton, William Holden, JOHN WESLEY
London: Macmillan and Co., Limited, 1927.

Johnson, Samuel, TAXATION NO TYRANNY
The Works of Samuel Johnson, VI, 224-63.
Oxford English Classics
Oxford: Published by Talboys and Wheeler; and W. Pickering, London, 1825.

Lecky, William Edward Hartpole, A HISTORY OF ENGLAND IN THE EIGHTEENTH CENTURY
Second Edition, Revised; eight volumes
London: Longmans, Green, and Co., 1879-90.

Leger, Augustin, WESLEY'S LAST LOVE
London: J. M. Dent & Sons, Ltd., 1910.

LIFE AND LETTERS OF JAMES MARTINEAU
In two volumes
New York, 1902.

Milton, John, PARADISE LOST
The Student's Milton, edited by F. A. Patterson
New York: F. S. Crofts & Co., 1930.

MINUTES OF THE METHODIST CONFERENCES FROM THE FIRST, held in London, by the Late Rev. John Wesley, A. M., in the Year 1744
Volume one
London: The Conference Office, 1812.

Moore, Henry, THE LIFE OF THE REV. JOHN WESLEY, A. M.
In two volumes
New York: N. Bangs and J. Emory, 1824.

Osborn, G., (Editor), THE POETICAL WORKS OF JOHN AND CHARLES WESLEY
In thirteen volumes
London: Wesleyan-Methodist Conference Office, 1868.

Simon, John Smith, JOHN WESLEY AND THE ADVANCE OF METHODISM
London: The Epworth Press, 1925.

Southey, Robert, THE LIFE OF WESLEY AND THE RISE AND PROGRESS OF METHODISM
Edited by Maurice H. Fitzgerald
In two volumes
London: Humphrey Milford, 1925.

Stephen, Leslie, ENGLISH LITERATURE AND SOCIETY IN THE EIGHTEENTH CENTURY
Ford Lectures, 1903.
London: Smith, Elder and Co., Duckworth and Co., 1907.

Telford, John, THE LIFE OF JOHN WESLEY
Revised
London: The Epworth Press, 1924.

Thomas, W., LE POETE EDWARD YOUNG (1683-1765) Etude sur sa Vie et ses Oeuvres
Paris: Librarie Hachette et Cie, 1901.

Thompson, D. D., JOHN WESLEY AS A SOCIAL REFORMER
New York: Eaton & Mains, 1898.

Trevelyan, The Right Hon. Sir George Otto, Bart., THE AMERICAN REVOLUTION
New Edition; Volume III
New York: Longmans, Green, and Co., 1909.

Tyerman, The Rev. Luke, THE LIFE AND TIMES OF THE REV. JOHN WESLEY, M. A., FOUNDER OF THE METHODISTS.
In three volumes
New York: Harper and Brothers, 1872.

Walton, Izaak, LIVES
London: Henry Washbourne, 1845.

Warner, Wellman J., THE WESLEYAN MOVEMENT IN THE INDUSTRIAL REVOLUTION
New York: Longmans, Green, and Co., 1930.

WESLEY STUDIES, by Various Writers
London: Charles H. Kelly, 1903.

Wesley Historical Society PROCEEDINGS

Wesley Historical Society PUBLICATIONS

Whitehead, John, THE LIFE OF THE REV. JOHN WESLEY, M. A.
Philadelphia: William S. Stockton, 1845.

Winchester, C. T., THE LIFE OF JOHN WESLEY
New York: The Macmillan Company, 1906.

THE WORKS OF EDWARD YOUNG, D. D.
In three volumes
London: 1813.

BOOKS BY JOHN WESLEY

This list includes only those works which are described in some detail in the present study, and those to which specific reference is made in the notes. Pieces to which incidental reference is made may be found in the indicated portions of the complete WORKS (see *ante* under "Emory"). In order to facilitate consultation of sources where rare books are concerned, I have, when possible, made double reference to the original and to its appearance in the WORKS.

THE ARMINIAN MAGAZINE: CONSISTING OF EXTRACTS AND ORIGINAL TREATISES ON UNIVERSAL REDEMPTON
Volumes 1-15 (1778-1792).

A CALM ADDRESS TO OUR AMERICAN COLONIES
A New Edition, Corrected and Enlarged
Bristol: William Pine, 1775.

A CHRISTIAN LIBRARY: CONSISTING OF EXTRACTS FROM, AND ABRIDGMENTS OF, THE CHOICEST PIECES OF PRACTICAL DIVINITY WHICH HAVE BEEN PUBLISH'D IN THE ENGLISH TONGUE
In fifty volumes
Bristol: Felix Farley, 1749-55.
(Same title)
In thirty volumes
London: T. Blanshard, 1819.

(NOTE: In describing THE CHRISTIAN LIBRARY I have borne in mind the first of these editions. In giving references I have invariably mentioned the second edition, since it was derived from Wesley's corrected copy. The reasonableness of this procedure will, I trust, be obvious.)

A COLLECTION OF HYMNS FOR THE USE OF THE PEOPLE CALLED METHODISTS
The sixth edition
London: The New Chapel, 1788.
(NOTE: The foregoing publication contains the Preface of 1780. I have not seen a first edition.)

A COLLECTION OF MORAL AND SACRED POEMS FROM THE MOST CELEBRATED ENGLISH AUTHORS
In three volumes
Bristol: Felix Farley, 1744.

THE COMPLETE ENGLISH DICTIONARY, EXPLAINING MOST OF THOSE HARD WORDS, WHICH ARE FOUND IN THE BEST ENGLISH WRITERS
Bristol: William Pine, 1764.

A CONCISE ECCLESIASTICAL HISTORY, FROM THE BIRTH OF CHRIST TO THE BEGINNING OF THE PRESENT CENTURY
In four volumes
London: J. Paramore, 1781.

A CONCISE HISTORY OF ENGLAND, FROM THE EARLIEST TIMES, TO THE DEATH OF GEORGE II
In four volumes
London: Robert Hawes, [no date, but] 1776.

AN EXTRACT FROM DR. YOUNG'S NIGHT THOUGHTS ON LIFE, DEATH AND IMMORTALITY
Bristol: William Pine, 1770.

AN EXTRACT FROM MILTON'S PARADISE LOST
With Notes
London: Henry Fenwick, 1763.

THE HISTORY OF HENRY, EARL OF MORELAND
London: J. Paramore, 1781.

HYMNS AND SPIRITUAL SONGS, INTENDED FOR THE USE OF REAL CHRISTIANS OF ALL DENOMINATIONS
The Second Edition
London: Henry Cock, 1754.

THE JOURNAL OF THE REV. JOHN WESLEY, A. M.
Standard Edition, eight volumes, Nehemiah Curnock editor
London: Robert Culley, 1909-16.

THE LETTERS OF THE REV. JOHN WESLEY, A. M.
Standard Edition, eight volumes, John Telford editor
London: The Epworth Press, 1931.

SACRED HARMONY, OR A CHOICE COLLECTION OF PSALMS AND HYMNS, SET TO MUSIC IN TWO AND THREE PARTS: FOR THE VOICE, HARPSICHORD & ORGAN
[No date, but probably] 1781.

SELECT HYMNS DESIGNED CHIEFLY FOR THE USE OF THE PEOPLE CALLED METHODISTS
Second Edition, Corrected and Enlarged
London: 1765.
SACRED MELODY, OR A CHOICE COLLECTION OF PSALM AND HYMN TUNES. With a Short Introduction.
(NOTE: The two foregoing items were invariably bound together.)

SELECT PARTS OF MR. HERBERT'S SACRED POEMS
London: R. Hawes, 1773.

A SHORT ACCOUNT OF THE LIFE AND DEATH OF THE REV. JOHN FLETCHER
New York: William Durell, 1795.

A SURVEY OF THE WISDOM OF GOD IN THE CREATION: OR, A COMPENDIUM OF NATURAL PHILOSOPHY
In five volumes
The Third Edition, Enlarged
London: J. Fry and Co., 1777.

INDEX

www.ingramcontent.com/pod-product-compliance
Lightning Source LLC
LaVergne TN
LVHW020628100826
845148LV00012B/2093

9781556357923